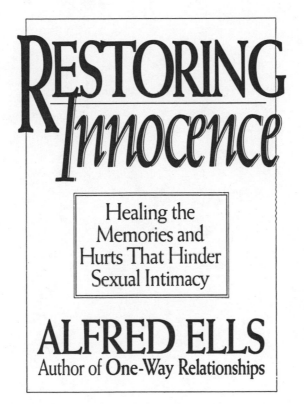

RESTORING Innocence

Healing the Memories and Hurts That Hinder Sexual Intimacy

ALFRED ELLS
Author of One-Way Relationships

RESTORING
Innocence

ALFRED ELLS
Author of One-Way Relationships

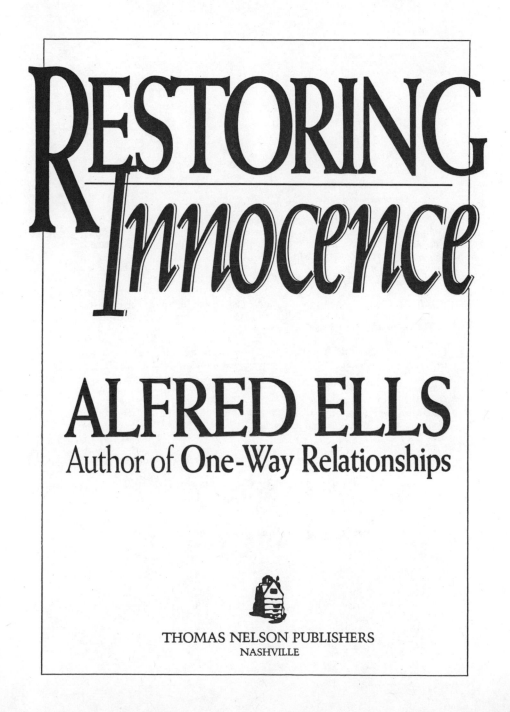

THOMAS NELSON PUBLISHERS
NASHVILLE

The names of the persons whose stories are told in this book have been changed to protect their identities, unless they have granted permission to the author or publisher to do otherwise. All other identities are concealed as composites of several case histories.

Published in Nashville, Tennessee, by Thomas Nelson, Inc., and distributed in Canada by Lawson Falle, Ltd., Cambridge, Ontario.

Printed in the United States.

Scripture quotations are from THE NEW KING JAMES VERSION of the Bible, unless otherwise noted. Copyright 1979, 1980, 1982, Thomas Nelson, Inc., Publishers.

Scripture quotations noted KJV are from the KING JAMES VERSION.

References marked TLB are from *The Living Bible* (Wheaton, Illinois: Tyndale House Publishers, 1971), and are used by permission.

Library of Congress Cataloging-in-Publication Data

Ells, Alfred.
   Restoring innocence / Al Ells.
     p.   cm.
   ISBN 0-8407-7453-2
   1. Sex in marriage—United States. 2. Sex. 3. Sex—Religious aspects—Christianity. I. Title.
   HQ18.U5E53 1991
   306.7—dc20
                                   90–26628
                                     CIP

*To a sexually
wounded
generation that
has lost its
innocence and
needs
restoration.*

Contents

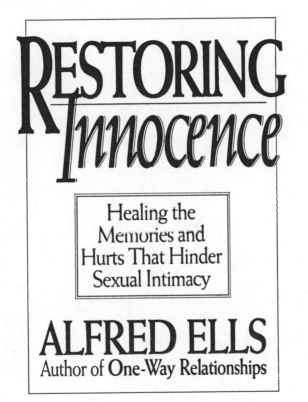

RESTORING Innocence

Healing the Memories and Hurts That Hinder Sexual Intimacy

ALFRED ELLS
Author of **One-Way Relationships**

Foreword

*T*he last thing in the world I wanted to do was to have that discussion—*again!* If Al and I had another of those "talks" about sex, I thought I would scream, and I knew he felt the same way. Finally, in desperation, I turned to him and said in a rare moment of insight and honesty, "Honey, face it. When you married me, you got damaged goods."

Al stared at me speechless for a moment, then said, "I know, so did you." So began our personal examination of what to do with all the wounds. With time and tears, we both came to know that the Lord did have answers to our painful questions and that His answers are available for *all* who are hurting and damaged.

My husband, Al, is my best friend, my gracious lover, and my close confidant. We have been married for twenty years, and as we have faced and resolved our sexual pasts, we have reaped untold benefits. I can say to you without reservation: the memories and hurts that hinder sexual intimacy can be healed.

I remember Al coming home one day from his

counseling practice emotionally weighed down and exhausted. As we talked, he agonized over the many, many people he sees daily who carry the pain of sexual wounds. He said, "If only more people could know that healing and restoration are available."

Immediately I said, "You need to teach a class and share what you have learned. I know God will bless it." The classes that resulted have been life-changing for hundreds of people. For the second time, he has put his material into a book, making it, in many ways, the culmination of two specific needs: our personal need for healing and help in our own marriage, and the need of so many hurting and confused people we have met who are seeking healing too.

Al and I have found that the Lord is intensely interested and continually active on our behalf. As we have lived out the principles of His healing, we have gained a rich harvest of love and joy.

As you open this book, I want you to know this: God is concerned and cares about you, and He has answers individually designed for you and your need.

If you will use this book to face yourself and face God, I believe you can find the deep fulfillment and sexual intimacy you desire.

Susan Ells
September 1990

Introduction

*T*he *American Heritage Dictionary* defines *innocence* as the quality of being "uncorrupted by wrongdoing." It comes from the Latin word *innocens*, meaning "not harmful." Sexual innocence does not mean being sexually naive, but, more appropriately, means not having been sexually harmed.

After years of walking thousands of people through their pain, I am convinced that there are countless others who need to experience a restoration of innocence—a restoration to the truth that sex can be pleasurable and harmless to us and to others.

Sexual love, in order to be truly fulfilling, needs to remain innocent. It should never risk long-term gain for short-term pleasure through momentary indiscretions. It should not violate another's boundaries or produce shame. When sexual love is wrongly given, the heartfelt feelings of completeness, closeness, and warmth are lacking. It is two bodies merging, not two souls touching. Pleasure may come but it is only fleeting, not fulfilling. Sex needs to be a vibrant part of an overall relationship of caring and commitment, but not the only part. The pleasure of sex needs to be balanced within the sacredness of healthy guidelines in order to achieve lasting and profound fulfillment. Sacrificing either only precipitates wounding.

This book offers God's path to pleasurable and sacred sex as well as life-changing answers for those who have struggled with sexual intimacy. Since most have been sexually wounded, it offers hope and healing to many readers who need the pain and shame removed from sex—healing of their sexual past, release from powerful family and first-love experiences that have caused the wounds, healing that restores innocence and brings true sexual fulfillment.

For those who have not been wounded, these pages provide insight into what is needed to help others, whether they're friends, neighbors, or family members.

Restoring Innocence is about our sexual roots and heritage. It is an in-depth look at the personal heartache most of us secretly experience with sex and also a handbook on how healing works and what you can do to have innocence—yours or someone else's—restored. Most importantly, it is a testimony of how much God cares. When sex becomes painful and shame makes us cower, he is near. It is his touch that is available to remove the harm, heal the hurts, and restore our innocence.

Bless you!

Alfred Ells
September 1990

Chapter 1

HOW MUCH SEX IS ENOUGH?

"She looked me right in the eye and said, 'I'd rather eat a good cheeseburger.' I was stunned. I couldn't believe what I was hearing. I asked her again, 'You mean you'd rather eat than have sex?'

"Without hesitating, she answered, 'Yes. There are a lot of times I just go through the motions to please you but I would enjoy a burger more!'"

Ryan sat on the edge of his chair recounting the traumatic conversation with his wife, Ann. "I still didn't believe her so I asked again, 'Do you mean you really don't like sex that much? Are you telling me that you have always felt this way?'

"She then told me, 'Yes. There have been countless times that I just gave you sex to keep you happy—to keep you from getting mad at me.'

"My worst fear had come true. I didn't know what to say. The silence was horrible as we sat there, not moving. My thoughts raced through the fights we'd had over sex. Just last month I had gotten angry at her for wanting to read a novel instead of making love. Before that I had been upset because we had not had sex before I left town for a few days. And there was the time she wanted to watch a TV program when I wanted to make love. On Sundays she always wanted an afternoon nap when I wanted sex. Over and over again, it was the same old story: my wanting sex, her wanting something else.

"Then she added the clincher: 'I'm not saying I don't ever enjoy sex with you, I'm just saying that I don't enjoy it as often as you do. I'm not a red-hot tomato. I don't want sex all the time, and I have trouble enjoying it. I think my past has affected me, but that doesn't mean I don't like it at all. You're going to have to learn to accept me just the way I am.'

"When she finished, she got up and left the room. I knew you were her counselor, so I thought I would call you for an appointment."

Ryan's story is a common one: A husband married to a wife who doesn't want sex as much as he does. It's also common for this tension to erupt in conflict, even to the point of serious confrontation like Ann's.

Because of her family life and first sexual experiences, she had been left with a painful sexual legacy that she was just beginning to face. Her uncle had molested her when she was a little girl, and her early family life had not been conducive to forming a healthy perspective of sex. Consequently, she had developed a long-standing pattern of giving sex to get love, rarely enjoying it at all. Now, however, she was getting honest with Ryan about her feelings and problems. But Ryan was having difficulty accepting the limitations this imposed.

"Are you wanting to talk about what we can do for Ann, or what we can do for you?" I asked.

"I'm not sure," he replied.

"We both know that Ann has a problem she's

*It was not just an issue
of Ann's not wanting
sex enough; it was also
a major problem of Ryan's
wanting too much sex
for the wrong reasons.*

working through, but you also seem to have a problem." He stiffened in the chair as I continued, "You are the one who came today for help, not Ann. I am wondering if you are the one who is really hurting about this."

I had struck a nerve. He shifted in the chair and turned around as if looking for an escape. "I guess I never thought about it that way," he responded. "It does bother me a lot and I don't know what to do about it. I was hoping you could help her and things would get better."

"Ryan, I can only help her as she wants me to. I can help you now if you will let me."

After a long silence, he asked, "How can you help me?"

"By helping you see why you are hurting so much about this. Also by helping you let go of the disappointment and desperation you must be feeling."

Tears welled up in his eyes, but instead of allowing himself to cry, he got angry, blaming Ann for the problem. He remained unwilling to face his own hurt or contribution. He left the session upset but committed to returning. I knew it would take more time and softening before he could admit to the hurt beneath his anger.

Sex had always been powerful yet painful territory for Ryan. He retained vivid memories of his childhood sexual experiences. When he was eight, his mother caught him playing "nasties" with the little girl next door. It shamed *her* so deeply that she immediately marched him down to the church so he could confess to the priest. He swore he would never do it again, but every kid in the neighborhood played "nasty." The peer pressure and curiosity won out.

Though he never got caught again, he still felt guilty and ashamed.

The older he got, the more conflicting messages he received about sex. The church and his mom reinforced the belief that sex was special, but only within marriage. All the guys at school said he would be stupid to wait—a man was supposed to have "experience" before marriage and the more the better. In the culture of his small town, a man's identity and worth were wrapped up in the ability to drink, work, and conquer women. The pressure for sex was always there.

When Ryan did come back for counseling, I asked him about his first love.

"Her name was Betty. She was a junior and I was a sophomore in high school."

"What did you like about her?"

"She was cute and fun loving. She had a way of making things more exciting."

"Did you sleep with her?" I questioned.

"No. I didn't," his eyes watered. "I really loved her and we wanted to save sex for marriage. We went together for three years and only petted."

"Why did you break up?"

"We had a fight just before I went into the hospital for an operation. She never came to visit me or even called. I was so hurt. I waited for her to call after I got out. The next thing I heard she was dating some other guy, and within a few months, she was pregnant. She always teased me about finding someone else, but I never thought she'd do it." Tears slowly crept down his face.

"How did that make you feel?" I asked.

"I was really upset. I had done everything I could to keep her a virgin like she wanted. And then she went and gave herself to somebody else she hardly knew." The angry tears came faster. His breathing accelerated. He looked like a dam ready to break.

"It sounds like she really hurt you. She broke your heart."

Then the flood came. He sobbed loudly, uncontrollably, his chest heaving with the weight of the pain. He wailed and wailed as the hidden hurt of a broken heart was finally let out.

Sexual surrender is powerful stuff. Betty's surrender to someone other than him left him feeling cheated and rejected. In the act of making love, men possess and women surrender to the possessing. For a man, sex is a deep validation of his masculinity. The woman's willingness to be possessed by him is an affirmation of how much value and worth he holds in her eyes. Her invitation to be possessed can deeply enrich his inner being, and her refusal can deeply wound. And if bonds of emotional attachment have developed, her surrender to someone else can be devastating.

Betty probably had no idea that her surrender to another man would so deeply wound Ryan. She did not know the power of her own sexuality. She was just a young girl who gave sex to get love, not realizing how profoundly it would affect her life or the men she surrendered to.

When Ryan finished, he sat back in the chair, shook his head, and said, "I didn't know all that was in me!"

"How do you feel now?" I asked.

"Like a ton of weight has been lifted."

"It always feels good to have the pain of the past released," I reflected, "but carrying that pain all these years must have done something to you. After your experience with Betty, how did you relate to women?"

He instantly responded, "I swore I'd get the sex that was due me. Every time I went out with a girl in college, I pushed for sex. If I didn't get it, I did not go out with them again."

"Were you trying to make up sexually for the hurt you experienced emotionally?"

"Yeah. I guess so. I never thought of it that way, but as we're talking I can see how I may have used women sexually to make up for losing Betty."

"Were you also trying to prove something?" I asked.

"Maybe I was trying to prove that I was okay, that I was good enough for a woman to want me. I know it meant a lot to me for them to want me, even though after we had sex I didn't want them."

I risked a projection. "I bet you married Ann because she didn't surrender to you as fully as the others. Is that true?"

He looked surprised. "How did you know? She was the only one I dated who insisted we wait until we were married before we had sex."

The light of understanding was getting brighter. Since he did not trust women who surrendered too readily to his advances, Ann's self-control before marriage made him feel safe.

Ryan had vowed never to be hurt again, so he was afraid of giving himself to a woman. This made his romantic relationships a roller-coaster ride. When he was interested in them, he pursued with flowers, cards, and attention. When they responded, he had sex with them, then pulled away so he could not be hurt. And when they in turn withdrew, he redoubled his effort to win them back. He craved their intimacy and surrender but ran scared when it was given.

This is how the wound of *defrauding* works. Whenever one feels cheated out of what could or should have been theirs, the temptation is to redouble the effort to regain what was lost, all the while trying to avoid being wounded again.

After eight years of marriage, Ann had become distrustful of Ryan's affection because it usually meant that sex was next. After sex, Ryan just turned over and went to sleep. Because sex was void of affection, Ann was driven deeper into sexual indifference, all the while feeling that she was merely a sexual object to men. As a result, she practiced codependent sex, giving Ryan sex either to avoid his anger or to get attention. Eating a cheeseburger offered more promise of pleasure than sex with Ryan.

Most relationship problems are like this. Underneath the bickering and lack of communication is a wounded heart crying out for love. These unhealed wounds from the past fuel self-defeating patterns and vicious cycles of action and reaction. Ryan's wound was at the very core of their sexual and marital problems. Ann's wound also contributed.

Ryan's hurt triggered a pattern of giving love and attention to get sex. When men and women do this, they are not just wanting more good sexual feelings. On a deeper emotional level, they are trying to get their own need for love, care, or significance met through the sex. Somehow sex becomes their way of being valued.

Since sex is so powerfully validating, this is an easy trap to fall into. But healthy relationships require more than one way of showing love. Affection, shared moments, touching, listening, and verbal affirmations are all important "I care" messages. Giving gifts, doing favors, and spending time together are also ways to say "I care." A relationship needs all of these in balance, for sex alone does not provide emotional health. If sex is the only or predominant "I care" message, it will cast suspicion on all the other messages and create a sterile relationship.

"Do you really like sex a lot?" I asked.

"Yeah, don't you?" he answered.

"Yes, but I get the feeling that you put a lot more emphasis on sex than I do. It has obviously caused you some serious problems."

"What do you mean serious problems? I don't have any serious problems with sex."

"Your sexual practices in college caused you and others a lot of pain. And by marrying a woman who doesn't like sex so much, you have assured sexual unfulfillment. It seems to me that sex has not worked very well for you. Instead of being helpful, it has been harmful."

He became visibly emotional again, but thought a long time before answering. "You're right. Sex has rarely worked for me even though I wanted it to.

"I've never told anyone this before, but I have an ongoing problem with masturbation and pornography. I've also been involved with other women twice, back when we were first married. If Ann knew about them she would die."

"How do you feel telling me this?"

"Ashamed."

I continued probing, "Does that mean you really did not want to be unfaithful?"

"I never wanted to betray Ann's love, but the temptation was just too great. I couldn't resist."

"You couldn't resist what?" I asked.

"In both situations, they were women I worked with. They acted interested in me, and I just couldn't help pursuing them. But after we had sex, I felt so bad, I just couldn't stand the guilt of what I had done."

"So in both situations you were violating your conscience but still could not stop yourself," I summarized.

His eyes looked down and his shoulders drooped as he sighed, "Yes."

I continued, "Do you also have trouble resisting sexual thoughts?"

"All the time. They never leave me. I can't see a woman without thinking about her breasts or what she'd be like in bed. I can't stand it when I'm home on weekends around Ann. I'm constantly thinking about sex with her."

Ryan's problem was not just an issue of Ann's not wanting sex enough, but of his wanting sex too much. Sex pervaded his thought life and drove him secretly to pornography, masturbation, and adultery. Ryan's need for sex was controlling him rather than his being in control of it. It was becoming an addiction.

"How can sex be an addiction?" Ryan jokingly asked. "I thought sex was one of those things you couldn't get enough of."

Many people, especially men, have this attitude. It was one of Ryan's beliefs until he began to realize how his obsession with sex was hurting him.

The World Health Organization defines *addiction* as "a pathological relationship to a mood-altering event, experience, or thing that has life-damaging consequences."

Sex can be addictive when we give it too much power . . . power to control us. Sex controlled Ryan's thought life and therefore motivated much of his behavior. He could not dismiss these thoughts without a real struggle.

The power of an addiction is felt through the irresistible urge to act on the behavior regardless of the risk. Sexual addicts have an irresistible urge for gratification whether through masturbation, pornography, sexual involvements, deviant, or other behavior. And they will act on that urge, even though they know they are risking their marriage or health.

Most homosexuals I have counseled are sexually addicted. They compulsively risk their lives for one more brief moment of pleasure in spite of the threat of AIDS and other consequences.

Ryan's sexual appetite, like most addictions, was progressive. The addiction demands more and more of the object or experience in order to derive the same benefit. Just as one's body builds up a tolerance against alcohol, requiring more and more alcohol for the same effect, so sexual addicts require more sex, better sex, or even more varied sex, in order to derive the same fulfillment. This often leads to sexual experimentation and "kinky" sex. For Ryan, it progressed from *Playboy* and masturbation to XXX-rated movies and adultery. He found himself desiring hard pornography, when years before he would have been repulsed by it.

But addictions are not an "all or none" issue. There are different degrees of addiction, where a person can be mildly or powerfully addicted. Ryan needed to understand that he was not the "classic" sex addict, but that all the characteristics of addiction were operating in his life.

What Ryan needed to do was regain the power over sex that he had lost and quiet the obsessions. He also needed to realize that the sexual pressure he created in his marriage had to change. The law of love, not lust, needed to prevail in his home.

"How am I going to change?" he asked. "I've been this way so long I don't know how to be any different, though I must admit that since we talked and prayed about how Betty hurt me I seem less interested in sex."

"Ryan," I answered, "the obsession with sex will lessen as you do each of the following. First, overcome your denial about needing to give up your sexual obsession. Most people do not get better because they don't want to face the reality of their need to change. You are going to have to give up your dreams and desires for sex the way you've fantasized about it. Second, we need to discover and deal with the roots of your past that have empowered the obsession. Betty was only one of those roots."

"This is going to be hard," he responded. "I still go back and forth on why I have to change. I keep thinking that everything would get better if Ann would change."

"I know. That's the struggle most of us have. We would rather concentrate on the other person's weakness instead of our own. I think that is why Scripture tells us to take the beam out of our own eye before we take the speck out of our brother's. This also is why accountability to someone else is so important to your recovery."

Ryan agreed, and we began exploring his sexual, relational and familial past, looking for those contributing factors. As with most sexually obsessed men, Ryan did not have a healthy relationship with his mom.

His mother was unhappy in her marriage and looked to Ryan for emotional companionship. In so doing, she shared intimate thoughts and feelings with him that should have more appropriately been reserved for her husband. He also remembered incidents, even as late as when he was twelve years old, where his partially clothed mom would ask him to get a towel or an article of clothing for her. Her inappropriate nudity "sensualized" him—that is, it awakened his sensual desires before their appropriate time. Her mishandled intimacy helped set the stage for his future problems with women.

The emerging masculinity of a teenage boy is fragile. The foundation of how he views himself and women is established in relationships with mom and dad. And how young women respond to him cements these perceptions.

Whenever a son is closely and intimately bonded to his mother, it puts him in subtle competition with his father for her affections, stirring his natural desires to protect and possess. However, because he is not his mom's husband, both these desires will be thwarted and he will feel defrauded. This was the foundation for the powerful vows Ryan made in reaction to Betty's rejection.

Ryan continued in counseling and also attended a twelve-step, Christ-centered support group. The obsession with sex broke after we worked through the hurts that came from mom.

Ann continued in counseling. In the next chapter, I'll describe her wounded family legacy. Their sexual relationship improved, as did their marriage. Their patterns of compulsive and codependent sex were being overcome as the hurtful legacies of the past were healed. God was restoring their innocence.

It has been my experience that most men, and many women, have compulsive sexual practices, practices that are not fulfilling or healthy for relationships. Men try to get too many needs met through sex, especially needs that can only be met through emotional intimacy. On a deeper level they are really wounded, like Ryan, needing the experience of God's love and healing for their aching souls.

Whenever we attempt to heal our wounds with sex we only add more hurt. We make sex harmful to ourselves and others, because we become deaf to the wounded heart's cry for love that's beneath the compulsion. Sexually compulsive individuals need restoration to sexual innocence, where sex can be relaxing and pleasurable rather than painful and obsessive.

Chapter 2

INNOCENCE LOST AND RESTORED: THE GIRL WITH THE BLACK AND WHITE SOCKS

Sex is everywhere. It's talked about, written about, joked about, and paraded about to sell everything from cars and soap to fashion and food. It's the advertising by-line that grabs everyone's attention, saying, "If you're sexy and sensual, you will succeed. . . . If you are lonely, bored, unfulfilled, or having problems, sex will make you feel better. . . . If sex is good, the marriage will work." The lines go on and on. More sex, better sex, different sex—or even more, better, and different sexual partners—is the American dream, the ultimate pursuit of happiness. In other words, sex and sex appeal are what life is really all about.

But hidden beneath this veneer of smiling sexual glitter lies an entire generation of sexually wounded individuals. Consider the following facts:

- Thirty-eight million adults have been sexually abused.

- Two-thirds of all marrieds will experience the profound pain of infidelity.
- This year, one million children will be sexually abused.
- One out of ten women admit to having been raped.
- Date rape is alarmingly high—47 percent of coeds at a midwestern college have been date raped.
- Over 30 percent of all single, sexually active Americans have a sexually transmitted disease (i.e., herpes, venereal warts, gonorrhea, syphilis or AIDS).
- Arrests of voyeurs, pedophiles (adults who have sex with children), and exhibitionists have increased tenfold in the past decade.

And this is just the tip of the iceberg.

Our culture's passion for sexual knowledge and experience is not making us better, more caring lovers. Instead, it is causing more dissatisfaction, dysfunction, and pain. Most people I counsel, like Ryan and Ann, have stories of sexual conflict, disappointment, or shame. They have been wounded by the practices and beliefs of others or have been harmed by their own.

Homemakers, lawyers, office workers, salespeople, and other normal, everyday people carry the deep inner scars of hurtful sexual practices. They may appear whole on the outside but, all too often, are wounded on the inside. Like outer physical wounds, inner ones cause damage, and although seemingly invisible, they profoundly affect our lives. They cause us to practice *codependent* or *compulsive sex*.

The sexually codependent are the new generation

of "walking wounded," whose practices are the result of all those wounds. They are the ones who give sex to get love rather than enjoying sex because of love. Some surrender to the sexual pressures of others and later wonder why. Others retreat from sex, giving up or giving in to others' demands because it is just too painful to face. Both feel empty and sexually unfulfilled.

Those who practice compulsive sex are also dissatisfied and wounded—they give love to get sex but, like the codependent, are never fulfilled.

But though the statistics are frightening, they rarely reach our hearts. Let me tell you the story of one of these "statistics," a young girl named Eve, forever impressed in my mind as the girl with the black and white socks.

Eve's Story

She had it made—or so everyone thought until that fateful night. Beautiful and vivacious, at fifteen, she was just coming into the bloom of womanhood. Her sparkling green eyes and Arizona tan were set off by brown hair with red highlights. She made straight A's in high school and was a leader in her teen group at church.

Eve came home from school as usual that day, did her homework, and went to bed early. Her parents thought she seemed preoccupied lately, but they attributed it to pressures at school. About eight, a friend called and was told Eve had gone to bed early. For this friend, something did not add up—Eve had been withdrawing more and more in the past weeks. So she decided to go to Eve's house and tap on her window to see if she would talk. Peering in the window, she saw Eve stretched out on the bed dressed in her prettiest white gown, a Bible on her breast, hands folded, eyes closed. Eve was wearing one white sock and one black. The empty pill bottle was visible on the night-stand.

Eve's friend flew through the front door screaming. The paramedics were called, and Eve was rushed to the hospital. It was touch and go for a few hours, but she had been discovered in time.

"Everyone wants to know why you did it," I told Eve after she had been discharged from the hospital. She had been referred for counseling by the emergency room physician and consulting psychiatrist, and her parents brought her to see me.

"I'm not sure," she answered quietly, refusing to look up.

"Does it have anything to do with the black sock?"

Tears tumbled down her cheeks as she turned her head from me trying to hide.

"What hurts so bad that you can't talk about it?"

"I just can't. You'll think I'm terrible."

"Try me. It can only be less painful than what you've just been through. We all have secrets that we're ashamed of, but the shame will only get worse if you don't share the secret."

"I . . . I . . . don't know what to say."

"Just start at the beginning. What happened?"

She shifted back and forth in the chair, then began to tell me her story.

"I met him at school. He just came over and started talking to me. My friend thought it was great because he's a senior and plays on the football team. He wanted me to go to a party with him Friday night. I told him I couldn't because I knew my parents would not let me. He kept saying I had to go out with him, so we started meeting at school every day."

"Did you like him?"

"Yeah. He was nice to me."

"Did you end up dating?"

"No, but we did see each other at school all the time."

"How serious did it get?"

"We liked each other a lot."

"Did your mom and dad know that you were stuck on him?"

"No. I was afraid to tell Mom because I'm not supposed to date guys until I'm sixteen."

"If you liked him and he liked you, what went wrong? Did your parents find out?"

"It was something else."

"Tell me about it."

"He wanted to give me a ride home in his brother's car after band practice. I knew I shouldn't or I would get in trouble, but he kept telling me it would be all right. That we could be alone. I didn't know what to do so I got in. Then it happened."

The tears returned. She buried her face in her hands, not wanting to look up. I could feel the pain. I wondered what she was avoiding. I knew she had to face it or there would be no healing. Her suicide attempt had been a desperate try to avoid the pain and reality of something tragic, the black sock her own symbolic way of telling herself and others the truth. She felt dirty, tainted, something had happened which had left an indelible stain. I ached for her but knew we had to keep going. "What happened when you got in the car? Did he take you home?"

She looked for a tissue, then continued in a quiet

Something deeply private
and personal had been
violated. Something special
had been lost. She had
lost her virginity and,
with it, her innocence.
When sexual innocence is
wrongly given or taken, the
result is never positive.

voice without looking up. "We parked in an empty field near my house." There was a long pause. "He started kissing me and touching me."

"Did you want him to do this?"

"No. But I didn't know how to stop him."

"What happened next?"

"He started to touch me . . . down below . . . I told him no, but he wouldn't listen. He just kept on. He didn't stop. It was like a bad dream. It was like I was watching myself until he was done. I didn't know what to do. It happened so fast."

"You mean he kept pushing until he had sex with you even though you did not want to?" She nodded.

"I am really sorry that this happened to you."

The tears gushed again and her body shook. I now had tears in my eyes. Yet the empathy was turning to anger. What a tragic way for a young, innocent girl to learn about sex. What was the matter with him? Didn't he realize how profoundly his unbridled sexual desire would affect this girl? I answered my own question. No, he does not know or he never would have done it. He is just another sexually obsessed young guy who got his sex at the expense of someone else.

My thoughts returned to her. We now needed to focus on her pain and what she was telling herself about the event. Was she blaming herself? Did she see his responsibility? Did she realize that she had really been taken advantage of, even raped? What was adding to her pain? All these needed answering.

Something deeply private and personal had been violated. Something special had been lost. She had lost her virginity and, with it, her innocence. It was not something she had willingly and lovingly given. It was forcefully and unlovingly taken. The result was shame, guilt, and confusion. When sexual innocence is wrongly given or taken, the result is never positive, instead of becoming more we feel less.

"How do you feel about this?" I asked.

"Really bad."

"What do you mean bad?"

"I never should have done it. I can't look at myself in the mirror."

"So you feel guilty and ashamed?"

"Yes. It's all my fault."

"What makes you think it is all your fault?"

"I let him take me home."

We spent quite a bit of time sorting through the guilt issues. Like most people who experience sex in a hurtful or wrong way, Eve could not accurately figure out by herself what she was really responsible for and what she was not. She was guilty of deceiving her parents, and she had also not set clear boundaries. Maybe if she had loudly screamed no or been more assertive, he would have stopped. But at the same time, she was only fifteen. It is hard enough for adults to have all the boundaries for sex, love, and attention in a relationship fully worked out—especially if you never talk about them. Eve's family never talked. They were good people, but passive, as was Eve. Their parents had never talked about sex, love, or relationships, so neither did they. Which left Eve on her own to learn.

He was eighteen, but as unprepared for sex and a relationship as she was. He knew no boundaries either, therefore violated hers. She did say no, but he did not listen to her. Instead, he kept right on pushing for what he wanted. Like so many in our society, he was blind to what his sexuality was doing to him or others. His desire for the privilege of sex with a pretty young girl coupled with his inability to face up to the responsibility of it cost Eve her innocence.

Obviously, Eve was hurt by the experience. She no longer felt excited or good about sex; now, it was only painful and confusing. She needed to regain what she had lost and have the harm of this incident released.

"I feel different than I used to . . . I am not the same," Eve told me one day.

"How are you different?" I asked. Eve had been in counseling with me for three months.

"I feel like I lost something but now I've got it back. After it happened, I was so ashamed. I felt dirty. I didn't want anyone to know. And I never wanted sex again. But now I think I can handle sex at the right time with the right person."

Eve had indeed changed. She could still remember the incident, but it held no more shame for her. She had also grown in other ways. She now knew what boundaries were and understood their use and necessity. But I still had nagging concerns. What kind of man would she choose next? What would his influence be in her life? How would she handle her needs for love, attention, and affection from men? Did she understand how her family and first sexual experience were affecting her emerging femininity? These are questions every parent should consider and every woman should ask herself. Studies indicate that over three-fourths of all teenage women will experience sex before they are out of high school. What will this do to their lives? Especially with regard to future sexual practice and relationships with men?

Shaping Femininity

Family is the single most important influence in shaping inner attitudes about who we are and what we need. First-love experiences, especially sexual ones, are usually the second most powerful determiners of who we become and how we relate. We learn who we are by our involvements with others.

Eve's "lover" had unthinkingly involved himself in one of the most delicate developmental processes a woman goes through—that of determining and accepting her emerging femininity, called *feminization*. Feminization is the process wherein a young girl learns the feminine behaviors, attitudes, and feelings of a woman. This especially includes her sexual role and response pattern to men.

The involvement of men in a woman's life is crucial. When, where, and how a man becomes involved with a woman has far-reaching developmental effects in her life. Studies have also shown that feminization depends in large part upon a warm relationship with a father who encourages and responds to his daughter's emerging femininity. How dads invest in their daughters has everything to do with how those daughters develop and who they become. And a woman's first male love continues and refines the process. He will either help or hinder her unfolding womanhood.

Eve was in the "becoming" time of her life, growing into womanhood both physically and emotionally. She often received compliments from others such as, "What a beautiful young woman you are becoming." But like so many young women, the men in her life were diminishing her potential.

Eve's father was passive, disinterested, and uninvolved in her daily life. Overly dedicated to his work, he rarely talked to her and seldom showed her any affection. She was starved for his attention and, by extension, the attention of men. Her first lover gave her that attention, but in the process took much more than he gave. Possibly, if she had been more closely bonded to her father she would not have been as vulnerable. If she had received more attention and affection at home, it might have been easier for her to draw boundaries and protect herself from someone giving her that attention in harmful ways.

Whatever legitimate emotional needs a daughter has that are not met by her father sets her up to try to get those needs met in unhealthy ways from other men.

Giving Love to Get Sex and Giving Sex to Get Love

It has been said that women give sex in order to get love and attention and that men give love and attention in order to get sex. Both orientations are harmful. If women give sex only to get love and attention, they can end up violating their own values and beliefs. In violating those beliefs, they wound themselves and make sex less than it should be. Sex can become a subtle form of emotional prostitution, leading to compulsive or codependent sexual practices.

If a woman attracts a man by leading with her sexuality, telegraphing a message she cannot or does not want to fulfill, she will attract a man who is interested in giving her the love she wants in order to get the sex her seductivity promises. This establishes a codependent pattern of sex, which results in hurt and confusion not only for her but for the man who expects what the seductivity promises. And this pattern leads to offense and violated boundaries.

Conversely, if men give love in order to get sex, then they will invariably manipulate women in order to get the sex they want. This can cause violations which wound women deeply, while breeding disappointment and frustration in the man. Because sex and intimacy are disconnected for him, he will end up unfulfilled, wounding himself and not knowing why. To try to reach fulfillment, he will redouble his attempts, establishing a pattern of compulsive sexual practice.

These patterns and motives are practiced all too commonly. Sex and love become something we blindly pursue, not realizing the hidden motivations and long-term consequences of codependent and compulsive sex.

Because Eve was able to recognize the wound of her dad's inattentiveness, my concern for her future with men diminished. Had Eve terminated counseling without resolving her hurtful family and first love legacies, she would have been set up for repeated failures in relationships. Eve would have been tempted to give sex to get love, all the while feeling bad about it. She would have been attracted to men like Ryan, who give attention to get sex. In short, she would have struggled with codependency.

In *One-Way Relationships: When You Love Them More Than They Love You*, I share the following insights for those trapped in the pattern of codependency. *Codependency* is actually just a new term for the old problem of loving, caring, or giving too much for the wrong reasons. It's the professional term used to describe the tendency to:

- love in order to be loved,
- care in order to be cared for,
- give in order to get,
- please others in order to be accepted, or

- pamper and placate others in order to avoid consequences.

Most of us have some natural tendencies to be codependent. But for some, codependency becomes a powerful negative style of interacting that can deeply wound people and destroy relationships. When our primary motive for loving or caring for someone comes from our own desperate need for love, it becomes hurtful. We tend to give too much of ourselves in order to make sure others love us. Sometimes, we even violate and harm ourselves because we cannot say no when we should. Codependency is really a wounded heart's cry for love.

Open the Door to Healing

Sexual wounds and hurtful family legacies encourage codependent sexual practices and codependency. Healing is readily available if we will only open the door by asking God to show us how our families and past control our sex lives today. Give God permission to unlock the doors of memory, and have the courage to face your past. We all have wounded hearts crying out for love. By offering the wound to God, we are released to experience the love we so desperately need. Sex is not a cure for a wounded heart or waning relationship. God's healing and love are. Innocence is restored when the wounds are healed and the hurtful legacies resolved.

Chapter 3

HOW YOUR FAMILY
CONTROLS YOUR
SEX LIFE

"My family didn't have any genitals," said Ann.

The statement surprised me. I had never heard someone describe their family in such a way. "What do you mean?"

"I was watching a videotape of families when the narrator said some families acted as if they had no genitals. It instantly made me think of my family. No one in my family ever told risqué jokes or mentioned the words *sex, penis,* or *vagina.* I think we all acted like sex and sexual parts did not exist. But Ryan's family is just the opposite. They're always talking and joking about sex, so much so that I don't feel comfortable around them."

"Does that mean that sexual territory is embarrassing to you?" I asked.

Ann did not respond right away, she seemed lost in thought.

"What are you thinking?"

"I was just realizing how embarrassed I must feel

about sex. Even talking to you makes me uneasy. Ryan says I'm too inhibited. He thinks I should desire it more, but I don't feel I need sex that often. He also complains that I'm too squeamish about sex because I don't like foreplay or too much touching. He thinks something's the matter with me when I say I could probably live without it." Ann hesitated, "Do you think there's something the matter with me?"

I did not want to answer, knowing it would probably hurt. "Yes, Ann. I believe you may be experiencing a condition described as inhibited sexual desire, which means sex just doesn't hold for you the pleasure and fulfillment God intended."

Her expression changed. A few soft tears dropped from her cheek. Dabbing her eyes with the tip of a tissue, she said "I have always known it, but it's still hard to hear the words." She paused a few moments, adding, "Is it because of my family?"

"Probably. But not only because of your family. Sexual problems can have more than one contributing factor; but since families do establish the foundation of sexual expression, I am sure your family has contributed to the problem. Are you willing to explore how they may have done so?"

I asked for her permission because many people are hesitant to look closely at their family. Some people feel disloyal if they examine family weaknesses or share family business with anyone outside the family. As one family member in a therapy session aptly put it, "We just don't talk about those kinds of things with other people. We keep our business to ourselves."

It isn't necessary to broadcast family "sins and secrets" to the world. However, it can be unhealthy never to discuss family relationships when it keeps you from facing the truth about yourself and your family. Health requires reality, and an honest appraisal of our own and our family's deficiencies is part of the reality of life. They must be faced if we are to truly let go of the past and move on.

Family Power

Family is the single most powerful influence in shaping the way we relate to others because it develops within us:

- our self-concept
- our framework for love
- our view of others

Let's look at each of these in detail.

Self-concept

Self-concept is the sum of all the thoughts, images, beliefs, and perceptions we have of ourselves, and it is formed, in large part, by how our family related to us. If a family treats a child with neglect, ignoring the child's presence and needs, a feeling of not being worthy or important is created. In contrast, caring, attentive parents say by their actions, "You are special. You count. You are valuable."

How we see ourselves has a lot to do with how we relate to others. It also has a lot to do with what we expect from sex. Most women who have few sexual boundaries come from families that did not validate their self-worth. When this self-worth is lacking, there can be a tendency to give sex to gain validation—doing whatever is demanded in order to receive the love and approval so desperately needed. This is codependent sex. Tragically, it can invite sexual abuse and victimization. In the same way, those who place a lot of emphasis on sex and sexual prowess also usually come from families where self-worth wasn't validated appropriately. Acceptance and approval had too much to do with being sexually accomplished. People raised in these environments give love to get sex, wanting the validation that sexual prowess provides to counteract the insecurity felt deep within. This is what compulsive sex is. It can also lead to deviation and the violation of others.

How families validate, accept, love, discipline, or reject members can powerfully influence their inner self-concept. And this self-concept will greatly influence how one views body parts, sexual identity, sexual competence, and sexual expression with others.

Framework for Love

Family life imprints in each of us a framework for love. Your concept of what love is and how you give and receive it all come from family patterns of interaction. If the "I care" messages between mom and dad were devoid of any touching or affection with each other or you, two things may happen. You may have difficulty with touch and affection, feeling uncomfortable giving and receiving. And sex may not be easy or fully pleasurable. This is because sex is the total touching of two bodies, merging two people into one. It is the most encompassing physical expression of love that is possible. And where touching and physical affection were rigidly regulated, sexual constriction may follow.

The other possibility is that you may overcompensate by needing or giving touch and affection too much, and for the wrong reasons. Ryan gave and needed a lot of affection, but he always connected it with sex. He could not distinguish between non sexual and sexual affection—which are both needed for a healthy relationship.

When someone needs touch and affection too much, boundaries will be violated and the touch of the needy person will become more sexually oriented because sex is so sensual. The sexual needs may then supplant the common need for affection, leading to a pattern of giving attention to get one's sexual needs met. All the while, though, the real need for loving affirmation remains unmet. If the need for affection is not openly dealt with in a relationship, it can distort the fulfillment of other needs, causing a continuing void and resulting in compulsion. Sex is meant to fulfill our deep needs for affirmation and affection; but when it becomes the *only* means, it becomes too powerful and yields less fulfillment—not more.

View of Others

Our families also imprint us with a view of others and how to relate to them, determining what we will do with and for others. If your family treated men better than women, or sons better than daughters, then you will tend to value maleness over femaleness. If you are a woman in such a family, then it is possible that you will see your role as valuing the desires of men over your own. If your partner wants sex and you do not, then you will tend to defer to his desires rather than your own. The end result is that you will never consider your own sexuality or sexual needs.

If your family's unhealthy values offended you, however, then you may react by overcompensating. You may value women over men, femaleness over maleness, daughters over sons, and have difficulty being considerate of your husband's desires.

Either way, your family's perception of others will influence your relational and sexual choices. Sex will tend to be one-way rather than mutual.

Codependent Sex

As we already learned in chapter 2, codependency is the tendency to love, care, or give too much for the wrong reasons. Codependency also applies in the sexual realm. When sex is not mutual, one of the partners is usually giving sex for the wrong reasons:

- to not anger or offend the other person
- to make the other person like them or be happy with them
- to keep the partner from seeing them as deficient

Women who fake orgasms are practicing codependent sex. They are protecting themselves from being viewed as deficient. Also, women who only give sex to get love are in the same codependent trap. Good sex requires self-honesty and honesty with the other party; it requires mutuality. Not mutually perfect performance or desire—few couples have perfectly attuned sex—but mutual commitment to enjoy the gift of sexual intimacy that God has offered, and mutual commitment to foster a climate where both come to enjoy sex by embracing it for themselves and sharing it with the other.

Codependent sex, however, lacks this quality of in-depth honesty. In short, true intimacy is missing.

Intimacy is the profound feeling of enrichment that comes from the total sharing of one's inner being with another and the acceptance of what was shared.

It comes from the Latin word *intimus*, meaning "in-nermost." This pictures intimacy as the touching of two souls, the joining of two spirits. Intimacy becomes the soothing balm of our aloneness. When we taste of it, we are somehow less alone, less pained, and more whole.

In sex, we have the physical act of intimacy, which can bring an even deeper experience of oneness. Our physical nakedness reflects our emotional honesty, and our physical embracing shows our emotional acceptance. Profound and intimate sex does not require great expertise, but rather deep exposure of one's self and loving acceptance by the other.

With intimacy as the goal of our sexual expression, we can even experience differing desires and practices and still have healthy sex. A wife can still desire sex less than her husband, yet both can find great fulfillment.

When sex is codependent, however, the partners cut themselves off from the vulnerability of honest self-exposure, and they withhold the precious commodity of total acceptance. Sex then becomes more a reflection of the need for the partners to face themselves more honestly. Codependents must ask themselves these questions: Am I embracing my own need for sexual expression? Am I providing true sacrificial love, love with no strings attached? How vulnerable have I been?

But with the idea of sacrificial love must come a word of caution. When sexual and emotional vulnerability are offered and total care and acceptance are not returned, sex becomes damaging. Sexual vulnerability demands a sacred response, or it will shame and wound. Abusers, adulterers, and sexual addicts violate boundaries and degrade sex. They, too, are wounded individuals who need to seek their own healing. The codependent must realize that sacrificial sexual love will not fix them. Only God can. The codependent's continual sexual surrender will only feed the problem, not diminish it. One-way loving is rarely helpful or healthy.

Compulsive or Obsessive Sex

"I can't stop thinking about sex. It's always on my mind, even during church. My eyes and mind wander, looking at the buttocks of every woman in front of me. I used to think this was normal—that all guys feel this way—but now I'm beginning to wonder."

Ryan raised this concern during one of our sessions. Sex for him had become an obsession. Obsessions are ideas or thoughts that haunt us and cannot be shaken off. For the sexually obsessed, sex thoughts and fantasies continue for hours on end or throughout the entire day. While the unobsessed individual may have fleeting urges or thoughts, the sexually obsessed have let the fantasies take control. For them, sex has become so consuming that it is a constant companion in their thoughts, even the focal point of their lives.

Many families promote this kind of sexual preoccupation. They may joke or jest about sex or make frequent sexual innuendos. Or, on the other extreme, they may prohibit any sexual discussion and overreact to any sexual display. Both positive and negative overemphasis make sex too important. It will result in either sexual obsession and compulsive practices or cause children to want nothing to do with sex because it has been made too scary or powerful for them.

Also, when the family does not meet emotional needs adequately, children may resort to sexual self-stimulation in order to experience comfort. Sexually complusive individuals admit to feeling lonely all the time. This loneliness comes about in two basic ways. One is by not giving children enough attention, love, or affirmation, so they grow up seeking it through sex. And the other way is to give children too much love, care, or attention through enmeshment. When this happens, children will grow to adulthood craving that immediate intimacy they experienced, seeking it through sex when it isn't available.

Shame

Perhaps the single most hurtful legacy many families leave their children is shame. This painful emotion is at the root of most codependent and compulsive sexual practices. Where guilt says, "I made a mistake," shame says, "I *am* the mistake." Shame is often an excruciating and punishing awareness of one's own insufficiency and inadequacy, and it is probably the most painful emotion one can experience.

Not all shame is bad, however—a small amount is probably healthy. It can help remind us that we are fallible humans with a sinful nature and keep us from being a law unto ourselves. And it's also a valid emotional response when we have violated healthy laws and boundaries.

But too much shame can assign us to a life of fear and self-hatred, creating an enemy within that condemns and criticizes us. It starts an inner war that we rarely seem to win.

Both the sexually compulsive and codependent have that enemy within—a deep inner voice of rage, rejection, shame, or doubt that prohibits them from being at peace with themselves and their sexuality. And both have tied their inner feelings of inadequacy to their sexual practices. Sexually compulsive individuals try to feel better about themselves through sex, with some displaying an aura of machismo to declare outwardly what they wish was true inwardly. Codependent individuals also try to conquer their shame, but they do it by avoiding the anger of others or trying to win others' approval to reinforce their approval of themselves. Neither will be emotionally or sexually fulfilled until the hurts and pains of the past are resolved and the shame released.

Shame also adds to sexual dysfunction by increasing sexual inhibition. We feel too embarrassed about ourselves to be totally naked—physically and emotionally—with someone else. Our blemishes, fat rolls, and imperfections interfere with our acceptance of self and others, making us too self-conscious to be able to abandon ourselves in passion. Sometimes the fluids of sex can become embarrassing—the act of sex is then perceived as "dirty." Shame will declare too many do's and don'ts and restrict natural sexual expression.

On the other hand, a person may react against this powerful negative feeling by becoming shameless. Shameless sexual practices—promiscuity, prostitution, rape, incest, masochism, voyeurism, and pedophilia—violate personal and moral boundaries and cause hurt to one's self and to others.

Contrary to public perception, individuals caught in these vicious traps of compulsion and obsession carry a lot of shame, which is why many of them keep their sexual practices secret. They know their behavior would not stand the test of public scrutiny, they fear what others would think if their life-style became

Perhaps the single most hurtful
legacy many families leave
their children is shame.
This painful emotion
is at the root of most
codependent and
compulsive sexual
practices. Where
guilt says, "I made a
mistake," shame says,
"I am the mistake."

known. This causes them to resist facing their practices, which only increases the hold the desire has over them. Secret lives always breed shame and more sickness. The more shame, the more avoidance of change and the deeper and more secret the practice becomes. Bondage thrives in darkness. It wanes when exposed to the light of truth.

Shamelessness can also be seen in those who are overly open and vocal about their sexual practices. Those who loudly proclaim the virtue of unrestrained sex are probably reacting to their past, where sex has been embarrassing or shameful. These individuals are desperately trying to avoid feeling the pain of this very powerful negative emotion. This can also be true of homosexuals who participate in public protests for "gay rights." The protester believes that if others can be convinced that homosexuality is acceptable, then his or her shame can be removed. However, public acceptance cannot totally remove one's shame; only a profound experience of God's forgiveness and love can release one from its bondage.

Shame is, however, lessened by acceptance. The inner feelings of inadequacy you have are tied to how others validate you. If you experienced rejection as a child, you may become very shame-based, meaning that shame becomes a major motivation for what you do or do not do. All of us need acceptance and affirmation as children in order to experience worth as adults. Healthy inner beliefs about self and others allow us to be guided by conscience rather than emotional neediness and keep us from violating ourselves or others.

Next Steps

Shame is at the root of a hurtful family legacy and codependent or complusive sex is the result. We need to revisit the shaming events of our lives in order to be healed. This means that both the shameful acts of others against us, as well as our own shameful ways, need to be brought to the light of God's healing and grace.

"But I can't go to God and ask him to help me. I've failed too many times. I'm powerless over my addiction. I may never be able to stop this thing. I would feel like a hypocrite."

Those were Ryan's desperate words of hopelessness when I confronted him about his need for God. Many who are trapped in vicious cycles of compulsive behavior feel this way.

The victims of someone else's sexual practices can also feel hopeless and unworthy of God. Sandy, a victim of incest, doesn't feel God could ever forgive her even though she did not initiate or desire sex with her father. Because of what happened, and especially because there were parts of it that felt good, she feels dirty and undeserving of God's care and love.

Guilt and shame are sensitive territories to navigate. To get through them, you will need to separate the acts of the past into two categories: those acts committed against you—for which you had no responsibility; and those things you have done for which you do have culpability. It is very difficult to sort out this territory on your own because the feelings of guilt and shame are so powerful, powerful enough to cause denial, confusion, or exaggerated reaction.

If shame or guilt is part of your hurtful family legacy, you will probably need someone else to help you sort through these feelings and facts. Often this is your only assurance of not deceiving yourself and continuing in your shame and self-defeat.

So, your first step has been to recognize the shame.

The next step is to ask for help.

This takes courage because you will not want to relive the shameful feelings by telling someone else, but there is no other way. You have to be willing to revisit the shame in order to be healed. Choose a trusted and competent person who understands shame and also knows Jesus—the lifter of our shame. A spiritual awakening in Christ provides the experience of God's love, which is a powerful balm to the deeper inner pain of shame. For many, the fear of God keeps them from his love. But Jesus will come to you no matter what you have done or what has been done to you. He is the healer of broken hearts and the mender of hurtful pasts. We have only to ask.

Family Sexual History

The following questions relate to your family's attitudes and practices regarding sex. Exploring them will help you better understand the early family influences that have shaped your sexual practices. If you are unsure of an answer, give it your best guess. Being unable to answer the question can also be revealing. Pay special attention to your feelings as you examine each question. Feelings of discomfort or anxiety indicate areas of shame.

If you were adopted or raised by someone other than your natural mother and father, you may want to fill out this section on both sets of parents.

1. What are your earliest remembrances of sex?
2. When, where, and from whom did you learn all about "the birds and the bees"?
3. What were your father's prevalent attitudes toward the following? (Use one- or two-word descriptions.)

Premarital sex	Role of women
Marital sex	in sex
Masturbation	Nature and
Pornography	purpose of sex
Adultery	A man's penis
Oral sex	A woman's
Sexual fulfillment	breasts, vaginal
Role of men in sex	area, buttocks

4. What were your mother's prevalent attitudes toward the following? (Use one- or two-word descriptions.)

Premarital sex	Role of women
Marital sex	in sex
Masturbation	Nature and
Pornography	purpose of sex
Adultery	A man's penis
Oral sex	A woman's
Sexual fulfillment	breasts, vaginal
Role of men in sex	area, buttocks

5. What are your current attitudes toward the following? (Use one- or two-word descriptions.)

Premarital sex	Role of women
Marital sex	in sex
Masturbation	Nature and
Pornography	purpose of sex
Adultery	A man's penis
Oral sex	A woman's
Sexual fulfillment	breasts, vaginal
Role of men in sex	area, buttocks

6. Are your attitudes more similar to your mother's or your father's?
7. Did you ever witness sexual foreplay or sex

by your parents or someone else? If so, how did it affect you?

8. What judgments or vows about sex, sexuality, men, women, etc., can you remember making as a result of your parents?

9. Which, if any, of the following were found in your father's or mother's family line? Specify who.

☐ Adultery   ☐ Child molestation
☐ Masturbation   ☐ Bestiality
☐ Homosexuality ☐ Petting before
☐ Premarital   marriage
   sex   ☐ Coarse or crude
☐ Incest   sexual jesting
☐ Rape   ☐ Lust

10. Has some other person or member of your family had an influence on shaping your sexual attitudes and preferences? If so, who and how?

Chapter 4

THE FAMILY UP CLOSE: WERE YOU PARENTED, PARTNERED, OR PUT ASIDE?

Carol picked up the plastic figures and placed her husband a few feet from herself, her youngest son to the side facing away, her absent son right next to her, and finally her daughter next to her husband. I asked her to also place her ex-husband in the family sculpture. She immediately put him by her youngest son.

The tears started even before she stood back to look at her family. It was not at all as she had wanted. More than anything else, she wanted her family—the most precious thing in her life—to be happy, loving, and together. Yet the sculpture told the disappointing truth. She was having marital problems with her husband, her ex was still a problem, and her kids were moving farther away from her. The oldest son, who really understood her, had married and moved to another state. The family was breaking up.

Carol cried, and cried, and cried. She mourned the loss of her dream of a close family—one in which everyone got along, no one was offended, and everybody stuck together—one that could overcome any problem. We both learned that day that the dream of a perfect family can sometimes keep you from having a healthy family.

There was nothing wrong with Carol's desire for closeness, the problem lay with how she thought that closeness should be achieved.

Let's take time now to look at the need for closeness, what happens when families get too close, and what happens when they aren't close enough.

Closeness is a crucial issue in families. From the moment you were born, you have been learning how to manage closeness and distance within your family. As a newborn, you needed to intimately depend upon mom. In fact, studies have indicated that healthy newborn infants are so close to mom that they do not know they are separate beings. Then when you entered your "Terrible Twos," with its no-to-everything declarations, you began signaling an emerging sense of autonomy.

As you continued to grow, you needed to become more independent. Healthy parenting requires close and loving bonds in the early years, with progressive release and affirmation in the later years. How well mom and dad accomplish this transition sets the foundation for how the adult child will manage closeness and distance in relationships. Many adult relationship problems, especially sexual ones, reflect legacies of mismanaged family closeness.

Codependent and compulsive sexual patterns reflect unhealthy legacies of family cohesion. *Cohesion* is the technical word for family closeness. It relates to the emotional bonding members of a family experience with each other. When members of a family are closely bonded, cohesion and intimacy are high.

When the bonding is absent, there is little cohesion and intimacy, and members of the family are disengaged from each other.

We all need to live in closely bonded intimate relationships, but sometimes the closeness can be unhealthy, especially when it causes us to compromise our responsibility for self and others. When this happens, enmeshment has occurred.

Family Enmeshment

Families that bond too intimately are said to be enmeshed—they have become too stuck together, hindering healthy autonomy. This was part of the problem with Carol's family. Carol's son had been her support through the rough times of divorce and single parenthood. He was always there to listen and encourage, and through this emotional intimacy he became her favorite. When the time came for him to get married, they both had great problems separating. When members of a family are enmeshed with each other, it inhibits intimacy and bonding with others.

For the girl he married, this enmeshment meant that she had to compete with Carol for his approval, affection, and attention. Because intimate communication flows more easily between the enmeshed family members than between the married couple, Carol's son favored his mother more than his wife. When his job demanded that he move, Carol's son's marriage improved greatly. But many other spouses aren't so fortunate.

Enmeshment often provokes codependent behavior in the excluded spouse. She or he may increase loving, caring, or giving in order to gain needed love. Or the enmeshment may provoke increased compliance or control from the left-out spouse. Either way, the en-meshed relationship prevents the intimate bonding and oneness marriage requires, and, unfortunately, it is also often the cause of marital conflict and divorce.

Sexual expression is also greatly influenced by en-meshment. A son or daughter who has been too inti-mately bonded with one or the other parent is a set-up for addictive or codependent sex. The unhealthy close-ness tends to hinder boundary development and cre-ates insatiable needs for intimacy. Needs that begin to control.

Enmeshed Sons

Ryan is an example of an enmeshed son. His rela-tionship with his mother was so close that mom un-wittingly sensualized him. As I mentioned in the first chapter, sensualization is the premature arousal of one's sexual or sensual nature; it is the sensitizing of a person to his own or another's sexuality before the person is mature enough to handle the territory.

Ryan's mom frequently invited him into her bed-room to talk while she dressed. He had vivid recollec-tions of her naked breasts and party clad body. She also talked freely about "the birds and the bees" . . . too freely. Besides the sexual intimacy, Ryan's mom also victimized him through inappropriate emotional inti-macy. Sharing her heart with him, giving him con-stant approval and attention, telling him how special he was to her, she treated Ryan more like a husband than a son. This unusually close attachment caused Ryan to idolize his mom and make her the focal point of his life. With his greatest desire being to please her, Ryan dedicated himself to living out her dreams—never developing a sense of his own.

Because there was not a healthy transition from

dependency to autonomy, Ryan at twenty-two was still needing the constant affirmation, attention, and direction of a woman in order to feel okay. To fulfill this need, he pursued intimacy sexually and emotionally, seeking women who would let him get close quickly. His loneliness was diminished when he made love, masturbated, or visited prostitutes, but the good feelings were always fleeting. So, to maintain those good feelings, Ryan increased his activity, which eventually resulted in his becoming obsessed with sex. Ryan was caught in a vicious cycle, compulsively pursuing sex, and rapidly on his way to becoming a sexual addict.

Enmeshed Daughters

In the female equation of enmeshment, the daughter often becomes either dad's or mom's confidante and emotional burden bearer. When she begins to get involved with men, her relationships may continue in this pattern, promoting codependent sex. She will probably feel secure only when she's needed by someone just like dad or mom needed her. Attracted to needy men who rely on her willingness to help fix their emotional burden and loneliness, she will give sex to get love. She will tend to mother men, always going the extra mile for them and taking most of the responsibility to make the relationship work. This pattern of relating will set her up to be victimized by men who give love to get sex.

If she marries someone like Ryan, the relationship could end up being powerfully addictive. Ryan would offer her instant intimacy with his neediness, and she would respond by wanting to meet his needs, all the while reveling in his attention and willingness to be intimate with her. Ryan would have difficulty remaining intimate with only her, and he would want her to mother him like mom did—but only when he wants it. To get him to pay attention to her, she would redouble her efforts to please him. In time, she may either progressively assert control over him or, as an opposite reaction, become more of a doormat and cater to his every desire. Either way, life together will be an emotional rollercoaster. If they have children, she may get her emotional needs met through them and unwittingly enmesh them too.

Unless both of them realize how their families and past are still controlling their responses today, their dysfunctional patterns will be repeated sexually and relationally throughout their lifetimes.

Emotional Incest

Regrettably, enmeshment is tantamount to emotional incest—a parent's unhealthy attempt to find comfort and companionship by intimately bonding with a child instead of a spouse. Rather than truly parenting the child, the adult is partnering with the child, relating as if with an equal. Ryan's mom partnered with him, making him her emotional intimate. This intimate sharing stirred his sexual desires, as intimacy is supposed to, but the stirring of his desire without fulfillment created an even greater need for sex and intimacy, causing problems in adult life.

Even though he was not aware of it, Ryan had been violated emotionally and sexually by his mother's incestuous love. Though it had cost him his innocence, he found it hard to believe that her love was unhealthy. Part of the reason for this was the deceptive "payoff" that enmeshment usually offers. In Ryan's case, he received constant affirmation from his mom, and he genuinely enjoyed being her favorite. He came to idolize her, not realizing the sickness of the special status.

To find healing and have his innocence restored, Ryan not only had to be willing to face the unhealthiness of his mother's love, but had to recognize and relinquish the "payoffs" the enmeshment had brought him. This was the only way he could overcome the hurtful effects of the emotional incest—which, in many ways, could be as difficult to overcome as the damage resulting from physical incest.

Physical Incest and Molestation

Physical incest and molestation cause extremely deep wounds. Those who should be protective, nurturing, and trustworthy betray and violate the child instead. This is especially true when the molestation is done by a parent, older relative, or authority figure. This deep wounding causes immense confusion in the child as to what is normal versus abnormal and profoundly affects the child's view of self, sex, love, and relationships. The devastating effects are many, and they can plague a person throughout an entire lifetime. Let's look at the lengthy list.

1. *Damaged self-worth and self-image.* Sexually molested children will struggle with the issue of self-worth long into adulthood, blaming and doubting themselves for the sins others committed against them.

Children are impressionable; their inner being is especially sensitive to distortion and wounding. So they believe what they are told, which is why abusers frequently threaten, demean, and even blame them. This leaves children feeling bad and sinful, used and tainted. They do not feel worthy of another's love or even God's. Shame is always there for them: they feel like they are the problem, that something is profoundly wrong with them. Otherwise, why would this have happened to them?

2. *Emotional problems*. Incest victims have great difficulty controlling and living with their emotional life. They can be emotionally dead or shut down one minute and absolutely full of rage the next. Many experience the dissociative phenomenon of being able to "separate" from themselves and what they are experiencing. It was the survival mechanism they used during the abuse to avoid feeling the pain.

Chronic depression, mood swings, emotional deadness, anxiety, and even sleep disturbances can all be the legacies of incest. Each of these problems is a lingering expression of the unhealed wound. And until the incestuous wound is totally cleansed, it cannot fully heal.

3. *Relationship problems*. Victims of sexual abuse rarely manage relationships well. They have difficulty trusting others, often developing a pattern of emotional withdrawal or dissociation when the demand for intimacy is present. They may also become very codependent, doing whatever the other person desires or demands without regard for themselves or for what is healthy.

Sometimes they appear to be outgoing and gregarious, but this can be deceptive. Many remain inwardly closed, not wanting to share their innermost thoughts or feelings with anyone. Above all, they do not want to be vulnerable.

Vulnerable comes from the Latin word *vulnare*, which means "open to be wounded." Abused persons do not want to be wounded again—they can't even risk it. The fear of being vulnerable will cause them to respond in ways that sabotage intimacy and true oneness in marriage.

4. *Sexual problems*. Obviously sex is going to be an area of deep confusion and difficulty. Victims of abuse may become extremely promiscuous, confusing sex with love. Though they are sexually active, they may not enjoy it. They rarely have respect for their bodies, feeling no ownership for their own sexuality . . . their bodies belong to anyone who wants them.

Sex can also carry great shame and guilt, which will prevent them from ever giving themselves permission to enjoy sex. "Since sex was so wrong before, how could it ever be right?" will be their belief. If there were times during the incest that they experienced pleasure, there will be haunting shame and reluctance to ever feel pleasure again. They are afraid it would validate the fears that they caused the abuse.

5. *Physical problems*. Sexual incest and abuse are physically and emotionally painful for children. Later in life they associate pain with sex, even the very mention of sex. Vaginismus (vaginal contractions) and dyspareunia (painful sex) are frequent results. Headaches, muscle aches, or other signs of discomfort can be psychological manifestations of the unresolved emotional and physical pain. It is as though the pain was stored up in the victim's body and is seeking a release.

Emotional incest, physical incest, and sexual abuse are powerful stuff. All have at their root the unhealthy existence of enmeshment. Signs of enmeshment should warn a family that something immensely important has been ignored. And usually what's been ignored is an unhealthy marriage—one in which intimate bonding and autonomy are not working. If the problems are not rectified, the results will be passed on to future generations.

Ending Enmeshment

If you are in an emotionally enmeshed relationship, it is not too late to change. Recognition is half the battle. The next step is honesty with yourself and the other person. Relinquishing the "payoff" you have been receiving from the relationship will provide you with the strength to honestly deal with the other person and find your freedom.

If you are the initiator of the enmeshment you need to make amends. If you are the victim, you need to resist their control. Either way you will need God's strength. He has promised to fulfill all your needs if you will surrender to him. You will never be able to fill them all yourself. Yet if you do not surrender them, they will control you. You will constantly try to make people, places, or things fix your neediness. Many have found the following prayer helpful in "letting go and letting God."

Dear Jesus,
 I have come to see my need for love, care, _____, and _____. The things I have done to fill these needs have not worked. So I offer control of them to you. Please fill them according to your will and bring me peace. When I want control back, remind me of my inability and your sufficiency. Teach me, Lord, to trust you. Amen.

If you have suffered from an emotionally enmeshed relationship, the above-mentioned steps will

A common mistake
is believing that
"if we are real close
it shows that we
are healthy."
Another is believing
"I do not
need
intimacy."
Either extreme
is damaging
to one's sexuality.

help. Having someone talk and pray through the territory with you will also be immensely helpful. Because enmeshment can be a profound attachment of soul and spirit, a spiritual prayer of release is needed. Forgiving them for what they have knowingly or unknowingly done to you is also part of the process. But remember, forgiveness is not actualized unless full revelation of the offense against you is realized. This means that you will have to emotionally experience the hurt and anger the incestuous relationship has caused you before you are ready to forgive. Forgiveness does not deny reality; rather, it releases the penalty of hurtful wrongdoing.

Additionally, you will need to follow the guidelines given for healing hurtful memories contained in the following chapters. Your greatest challenge may be in finding the courage to continue seeking the healing God so liberally offers. Though healing is present, one must find and walk the path that leads to it. Do not give up or give in. If you do not grow weary, you will reap the benefits of your journey.

Family Disengagement

On the opposite end of the scale from enmeshment is disengagement—the lack of bonding that can occur between family members. Every family needs some disengagement so that the children can become independent, responsible adults who do not need the props of parenting to make them successful. Too much disengagement, however, is actually emotional abandonment. It breeds feelings of rejection in the child, who will then feel unloved, unlovable, or both. In adulthood, these people may either avoid bonding with those who are like the disengaged parent or, as an opposite reaction, try to capture the bonding and love they missed by seeking out those who are like the disengaged parent. The disengagement will leave a child needy and unprepared for healthy bonding. And disengagement, like enmeshment, also provokes codependent and compulsive sexual practices.

Ann's enmeshment with her mom was contrasted by her disengagement with her dad. When one parent is enmeshed with a child, the other parent will usually be disengaged. In Ann's case, her father's lack of bonding fueled her need to be close to men. She needed their love, attention, and affection to make up for what had been absent with dad. Unfortunately, codependent sex was the result.

She gave sex to get love even though she never fully enjoyed the sex. For her, it was only a tool she used to make sure men would like her. She was also afraid that not giving them sex would cause them to reject her, and, fearing their disengagement, she would redouble her efforts at sex and pleasing whenever they seemed disinterested or distant. Her relationships always progressed into one-way patterns of her giving and their taking. On the surface, she seemed to love them more than they loved her, but underneath she was loving them to be loved. She was a wounded heart crying out for the love she had never received.

Ryan's enmeshment with his mom was also fueled by his lack of bonding with his dad, who was critical and rejecting. His father's behavior drove him away from healthy interaction with men, causing him to need women that much more. It also made him less complete in himself. When sons do not bond with fathers, their process of male identification is hindered. A son learns how to be a man in great part by imitating his father. When bonding is lacking, the imitation process is thwarted and insecurity about his masculinity is bred into the son. To try to find his masculinity, Ryan used a woman's sexual surrender. His dad's disengagement fueled Ryan's tendency toward compulsive sex.

Patterns of enmeshment and disengagement with either parent can foster unhealthy patterns of codependent or compulsive sex. Ryan's brother was addicted to pornography, masturbation, and prostitutes. His desire for these practices ruled his life, costing him thousands of dollars and the shame of leading a secret life. It almost cost him his marriage when his wife contracted a venereal disease from him.

Ryan's brother had not been close to either parent. Mom had Ryan and dad had his work. Thus, Ryan's brother became the lost member of the family. His lack of bonding created a need to find solace and comfort from others who posed no threat.

Prostitution, a rich fantasy life, and compulsive masturbation were his safe answers. But his addictions represented not only unmet needs but unresolved anger. He was deeply jealous of Ryan. And as a result, he became resentful and jealous when expressing his sexuality. One of the prostitutes he frequently visited finally refused to service him because he handled her too roughly. His wife also complained of his anger.

Healing for most disengaged individuals, as for Ryan's brother, requires emotional healing and new learning. The past wounds of rejection need to be resolved, as do fear, anger, and jealousy.

Accountability is also a requisite of healing. Because it is hard for them to bond, disengaged individuals are loners. But new learning must take place with others. Ryan's brother needed to learn how to share his feelings, thoughts, and understandings of life. In doing so, he could begin to experience the intimacy and caring he so desperately needed. Disengaged people need individual and small group experiences of intimate sharing and caring. And they also need to experience the deep love of a God who is bonded to them.

Ryan's brother was a lonely, disengaged, and angry man. He could easily become a rapist, molester, or pedophile. The unresolved angers and jealousies had deeply affected his view of self and sexuality. His brand of sex, like his brother's, was not bringing true fulfillment. Sex for both of them was becoming harmful, hurtful to self and others. When sex becomes hurtful, innocence is lost because boundaries are being violated. Both needed restoration.

Chapter 5

Do you Remember Your First Love?

*E*veryone I ask usually remembers their first love. First loves are powerful initiations into the world of relationships. Their remembrances evoke nostalgic recollections of prom nights, fraternity parties, or football games . . . first kisses, special songs, or romantic walks. They can also elicit sad feelings and haunting regrets. Though first loves rarely last, their imprints may last forever.

An imprint is the legacy acquired from a relationship. Imprints from our first love tend to cement codependent and compulsive sexual tendencies that originated in our families. This is because the power of first love sets in motion healthy or unhealthy patterns of response to members of the opposite sex which dictate our responses in future relationships. Understanding imprints and recognizing yours can be the key to sexual fulfillment. Both Eve and Ryan were profoundly affected by their first loves. Healing for both came as they faced the imprint and worked toward resolving its power.

Imprinting

Raising baby ducks without their mother has taught us a lot about how animals, as well as people, develop their behavioral patterns. If the mother duck is removed just prior to the eggs' hatching and another animal is substituted, the ducklings will think the surrogate is their mother. They will bond to, and begin to imitate, the replacement. If the substitute is another duck, the ducklings will develop behavior appropriate to a duck. However, if the surrogate mother was a cat or dog, the ducks will never learn how to quack or waddle properly. They will pattern their behavior after the dog or cat instead of their natural mother. They will be odd ducks indeed!

These experiments have led to the discovery that ducks and other animals have developmental timetables by which they learn to establish and refine certain behaviors. Each species of animal has a unique crucial developmental period for imprinting or establishing a specific pattern of behavior. For ducks, the timetable begins shortly after hatching and only lasts a few hours. Whoever the ducklings bond to and imitate in this period of time will determine their lifelong behavior. It was also learned that the specific set of developmental behaviors could not be easily learned before or after the crucial time period.

This process of establishing behavioral patterns has become known as *imprinting*. The ducks are branded by whatever experience they have during the bonding period. Human beings also have developmental timetables, during which certain traits or characteristics are imprinted. What is experienced during those formative years lays the foundation for future practice.

Most sexually wounded
individuals have painful
first-love experiences
that wrongly imprinted
them and laid a poor
foundation for future
sex and love. As they
have recognized
their imprint and
brought the old
memories back
for healing, their
sexual fulfillment
has been enhanced.

This developmental principle has a lot to do with sexual choices. First sexual experiences and first loves imprint the person to behave in certain characteristic ways. Who you first bonded to, when you bonded, and how you bonded can dramatically affect your love life today. First-love experiences have a dramatic effect on the formation of inner attitudes about sex. What we say to ourselves about the other person, about ourselves, and about the experience will tip the attitude scale positively or negatively.

Most sexually wounded individuals have painful first-love experiences that wrongly imprinted them and laid a poor foundation for future sex and love. As they have recognized their imprint and brought the old memories back for healing, their sexual fulfillment has been enhanced. As I share with you the different characteristics of imprints, try to discover yours. When the memories come back and understanding develops, write them down. The steps in the chapter "Tracing Surface Problems to Root Solutions" will guide you in dealing with the memories.

If the memories are especially powerful, take your time and follow the steps given in the chapter "Healing the Memories That Hurt." Just as a word of encouragement, I have witnessed dramatic healing for those who are courageous enough to face their memories and, therefore, their past.

When Did You First Experience Sex?

I can only remember two people I have counseled for sexual difficulties who first experienced sex with their spouse after marriage. The hundreds of others first experienced sex before marriage as teenagers or even before that, being molested or victims of incest as early as infancy. Sexual experiences in childhood create profound confusion. Small children don't know what to think, and they are certainly not old enough to handle sex. Their imprint will be one of confusion and conflict, and it will affect them to this very day. They need to closely examine the experiences, prayerfully ask God to show them how the experience affected them, and further request the power to overcome it.

Most first-love experiences, however, take place during the impressionable teenage years—a crucial developmental time for sexual expression. If the imprint is negative because the intimacy was mismanaged, then sex will not work well in future years.

Teenage first loves are frought with ups and downs, fears, fantasies, and experimentation. This is the time boys become interested in girls and the girls are glad they are. It is a time of testing how relationships between members of the opposite sex work. The testing is healthy—as long as everyone follows healthy rules.

Teenage lovers are rarely mature enough to take full responsibility for their own behavior and the result of its influence in the life of another. Healthy relationships, by contrast, require that we assume full responsibility for how our actions may affect another. Teenage love is more of a playing at love than a full-fledged ability to love. Commitment is lacking, and emotions usually rule the relationship. When sex gets mixed into the relational experimentation, the consequences are rarely good.

The resultant attitudes and behaviors are frequently unhealthy, creating wrong inner evaluations and self-defeating inner promises regarding sex, love, and relationships. The unhealthy experience lays the foundation for codependent and compulsive sexual practices. Healing requires reexamination of our experiences during these crucial years.

Who Was Your First Love, and How Were You Treated?

In chapter 2, I shared how Eve's first lover was pushy and selfish. He gave her the attention she needed; but he extracted a high price in return. He invaded her, insensitive to how it might affect her emotionally or spiritually. The resultant negative imprint was so devastating that it provoked a suicide attempt. The experience made it almost impossible for Eve to consider sex pleasurable, men safe, or herself valuable. If not healed, this harmful imprint could lead to inhibited sexual response, promiscuity, or codependent sex. Since sex initially held no offer of intimate love and pleasure for her, she might perceive that it was only for the benefit of men, not her. She would give sex to get love, never fully embracing the gift sex could be to her. Rather than becoming an act of shared, meaningful intimacy, it could become a mere tool for getting all the love she needs.

Ryan's first love never became his first lover. By that I mean that they stirred up each other's sexual desires by long periods of petting and necking but never went "all the way." This created a lascivious imprint in Ryan. *Lasciviousness* is the stirring of natural sexual desire to the point of lust or obsession. Having his desire stoked without the benefit of completion caused him to desire sex even more. Then, when she rejected him and submitted herself sexually to another man, she deeply wounded Ryan. The resulting imprint pushed him in the direction of giving love to get sex so that he could get the release he had been deprived of. The sexual and emotional imprints made

Ryan concupiscent. To become *concupiscent* means to have an abnormally strong sexual desire. Ryan became obsessed with sex, which led to habitual masturbation, adultery, pornography, and compulsive sex.

In evaluating your first-love experience, it will be helpful to write out a description of your first remembered sexual encounter(s). In so doing, consider the following questions.

1. *Were you an eager and willing participant in your first sexual encounter, or were you pressured into it?* Many women experience their first act of intercourse under the influence of alcohol or drugs with partners who pressured for it or took advantage of their vulnerability.

2. *Were you molested as a child by a stranger or someone you knew and trusted?* You may not consider them your first "lover," however, the imprint of the experience will need examination. The same is true for childhood experimentation with other kids.

3. *Was he or she really considerate of your sexual desires and boundaries?* Boundaries are crucial to sexual fulfillment.

4. *Did your first lover make you feel inadequate, ashamed, angry, guilty, or fearful?*

5. *Did he or she put pressure on you to experiment in ways that made you feel uncomfortable or ashamed?* Oral or anal sex, as well as sex in public places, can be violating.

6. *Did your first lover share his or her heart with you or only his or her body?* Sexual fulfillment requires sharing both.

7. *Was your first lover patient, kind, and loving before, during, and after each encounter?* Or

was it a hurry-up affair, more lustful than loving?

8. *Did your first lover reject you or wound you
   deeply?*

9. *Was your first lover marriage material?*

How Closely Bonded Were You to Your First Love?

Bonding, or emotional attachment, affects the
imprint. The more closely bonded you were to the person, the more powerful the imprint. Ryan was head
over heels in love with his childhood sweetheart.
He readily agreed to her desire to avoid having sex before marriage because he loved her so much. This
made the later rejection even more powerful. If he had
not cared so much, the imprint would not have been
as deep.

One of the dangers of first loves is the intensity
they develop. The lovers can become totally absorbed
with each other in a relatively short period of time,
bonding quickly and intimately, which creates a
strong imprinting influence in both lives. It is not
wise to become intimately attached to someone until
you know him or her well enough to trust the result.
Mishandled intimacy causes wounding and dysfunction. Beware, teenagers and young lovers! Becoming
too easily attached too soon is a setup for failure.

Healthy attachment is a process that grows over
time, meaning months and maybe even years. A theo-
logian once wrote, "People are not supposed to fall in
love and get married, they are to marry and learn how
to love." Deep intimacy and bonding are to grow after
marriage, not before. Before marriage we are to explore the potential of the relationship through getting
to know the other without totally yielding our body,

soul, or spirit. Only the commitment of marriage can safeguard such surrender. Tragically, current dating practices doom many young people to being wounded. Within weeks they become sexually and emotionally bonded, which makes breaking up more like terminating a marriage because the bonding was so complete.

Such instant intimacy is more a sign of two desperate and hurting people than of a "marriage made in heaven." Each is craving intimate contact, thus revealing their own deep unfilled need for love. People who become instant intimates are susceptible to intimacy with anyone, their love hunger making them prey for anyone who wants to get sex by giving love. Once that susceptibility is imprinted, repeating the pattern is automatic. It easily leads to promiscuity, codependent sex, or compulsive sex. This is a persuasive argument for a "go slow and let it grow" attitude toward dating.

But it is important to realize that an inability to become bonded over time is also an unhealthy sign. It may mean that an individual has inhibiting fears of attachment because of a family background that fostered unhealthy bonding patterns. The chapter "The Family Up Close: Were You Parented, Partnered, or Put Aside?" offers valuable insight into family bonding patterns that set the stage for later first-love imprints. The inhibiting fears may also have been created by past wounding due to molestation and abuse. Because kids frequently repress such memories, the cause of the fears may be unrealized.

Examining how closely and quickly you bonded to your first love can help you understand yourself better. Were you afraid of closeness? Or were you craving the good feeling intimacy provided? Was it an approach-avoidance situation where you desired the intimacy but were also afraid of it?

Answering each of these questions can assist you in discovering how the attitude was developed. Knowing this can lead to change and healing.

The Problem with Good Imprints

There is a common, yet frequently unrecognized, aspect of imprinting that affects sexual fulfillment in later years. It is the difficulty of letting go of the good memories associated with past imprints. I learned this lesson when counseling a young wife named Tennile. She complained of dissatisfaction with her sex life. Tom did not desire sex as frequently as she did, and when they did make love, he was satisfied with thirty minutes while she wanted an hour. Tom enjoyed sex but felt he could never please her. So I asked her what she really wanted from Tom.

"I'd like it to be the way it was with Joey."

"Who is Joey?" I asked.

"He is the guy I dated for a year and a half before I met Tom."

"What kind of sex life did the two of you have?"

She blushed slightly at the question, but then answered, "I don't want you to think I'm really bad or something, because I dated him before I became a Christian. But we would make love every day for an hour or two. It was glorious. I had never had an orgasm before I met Joey. He made me like sex like I never had before. That's why it bothers me a lot when Tom only wants sex a couple times a week. I wonder if he really likes me. I also get to feeling real 'antsy' when I have to wait that long."

Tennile had a problem with too many "good memories" and an overdone sexual past. She and Joey had made sex the most important thing in their relationship. They both looked forward all day to the evening when they could enjoy sex together. This imprint of hyper-sex had set a false expectation for sex in marriage, and Tennile wound up comparing Tom's performance to Joey's and finding Tom's lacking. She wanted sex too much for the wrong reasons.

Codependent and Compulsive Imprints

As I got to know Tom, I realized his sexual desires were not severely lacking. However, he was beginning to give sex to avoid her anger, rarely enjoying the result. He would go to bed later and later to avoid the possibility of sex, or else fall asleep on the sofa watching television. This made her angrier, prompting him to give in to her sexual demands just to keep the peace. Her compulsive pressure for sex was provoking his practice of codependent sex.

This is the common pattern when one wants sex more than the other. The one who desires more sex pressures the other to respond. And the one who desires less responds to the pressure in codependent ways. Each feeds the escalating cycle of dissatisfaction. In order to break this self-defeating pattern, both need to acknowledge their contribution and examine how it may be connected to their first imprint.

Tom was a virgin when he married Tennile. At first, he welcomed her sexual desires because they made him feel loved and valued. He interpreted her deep need as true love. But when it turned to pressure and when she was not satisfied, he began to feel confused and insecure, doubting his sexual acumen. He even secretly assumed there was something the matter with him. Raised in a religious family, he had virtually no exposure to sex before meeting Tennile; she was his first love and lover. If she had not pressured so much, his imprint would have developed positively.

Exposing the compulsive and codependent pattern of practice brought a breath of relief to Tom. He was able to deal with his first imprint, ridding himself of the guilt and shame he was beginning to feel. Because they had both come for counseling so soon after marriage, it was easier to deal with the hurtful imprints and establish new ones.

Sexual partnership is a delicate adaptation of two individuals to each other. When prior sexual experiences are better than current spousal sex, the prior imprint must go. Ideally, sexual partners should imprint with each other, not with someone else. When you imprint with someone other than your spouse, you develop sexual response patterns attuned to that individual, not your future spouse. I believe this is one of the major reasons for monogamous sexual practices. Discontent in marriage frequently results from the inability of each partner to fully adapt to the other. During the developmental timing when sex first occurs, both are more able and willing to adapt to each other than in later years after much experience and other imprints.

Masturbation and Pornography

I believe most men, married or single, are hooked on pornography and masturbation. I am also encountering more women with the same problem of masturbation. Both are being controlled by their initial imprints.

Pornography easily stirs sexual desire in men because it appeals to the man's "eye-gate." Studies have shown that men are different from women in arousal patterns and stimuli. Touch and words are arousing to most women, whereas sight is a primary sense for arousal in men.

When young boys, out of curiosity, look at pornographic pictures, it begins to arouse their sexual desires and creates an imago—an idealized image—of what a sexual partner should be. Every person develops an internal picture of the ideal mate or sex partner. But the difficulty with pornography is that the created image is unattainable. The women who pose in pornographic magazines are not the average women in life. Additionally, their photos have been touched up and their poses are not the natural ones you will experience in healthy marital sex.

When pornography, or fantasy based on pornography, is paired with the physical arousal and release of masturbation, the resultant imprint dooms the person to future unfulfillment. There is no way that marital sex can compete with the unbridled passion of one's fantasy life or of the current plethora of pornography. Also, the depersonalization of pornographic material destroys the potential for emotional intimacy. And it is this emotional intimacy that brings the depths of fulfillment to sex, not the physical pleasure alone. Masturbation and pornography are self-centered ways to sexual fulfillment, devoid of intimacy and healthy relationship.

Healing for compulsive pornography or masturbation requires revisiting the early imprints from youth. Identifying the empowering core beliefs can open the door for change. There must also be a willingness to stop reinforcing the false image that has been created and have the current partner become the ideal of human sexual love and intimacy.

Healing Imprints

The specific steps for changing an imprint are delineated in the chapters "Tracing Surface Problems to Root Solutions" and "Healing the Memories That Hurt." In both you will see that recognition of the imprint is the first step. First loves and first sexual experiences are not often revisited in our memory unless we purpose to do so. I cannot stress enough the potential for change when one is willing to reexamine them in the light of new information. It will help you change your attitudes and develop new paths to fulfillment.

I have found that some individuals take to this type of analysis very quickly while others find it difficult. If you have difficulty remembering or analyzing, pray. Your willingness to ask God to help can be the crack in the door that will eventually open it wide. Also talk to other people you trust about what you are discovering. It helps to hear ourselves talk out loud about what God is revealing. Trust that God will heal whatever you are willing to have revealed. Restoring innocence requires facing the old imprints, erasing their effect in your life, and establishing your sexuality anew.

Chapter 6

SEDUCED, DEFRAUDED, AND VICTIMIZED

*T*he audience was so quiet that the silence was palpable. I began to doubt whether it had been such a good idea to teach on the dynamics of seduction and victimization to one hundred fifty women. Hurriedly, I asked them to bow their heads so that we could pray and dismiss. As I prayed, I asked for healing for the hidden roots of the past that had empowered the hurtful dynamics. A quiet sob started to my right, followed by a louder one toward the back. Within seconds, weeping audibly filled the entire room. My eyes moistened as I sensed the pain they all felt. Each tear shed was a realization of their own victimization and its effects.

I have come to believe that everybody is both a victim and a perpetrator. Some just more so than others. A sexually damaged woman who was victimized by an uncle through molestation will victimize the spouse she marries, in that he will be defrauded of the full potential of God's gift of sexual expression. Her victimization causes his victimization. A compulsively driven sex addict will victimize the women in his life. But the roots of his compulsiveness come from being defrauded as a child. And the women he victimizes will continue the cycle.

This vicious cycle of victim and victimizer is a hard one to face. Nobody wants to see themselves as a victimizer (perpetrator) of others. It is much easier to see ourselves as the victim of someone else's actions than face our own contribution.

There are also those who do not want to say they have been victimized, much less admit to hurting others. They do not want others to know their true feelings, and maybe they themselves don't want to know them either.

And, at last, there are those who say they have been victimized and seem stuck in it. They wear the victim label, feeling powerless to do anything about it.

In this chapter I want to talk to all of us. Sexual fulfillment has much to do with what happened to us (how we were victimized) and how we have responded in return (how we victimize self and others). The dynamics of seduction, victimization, and defrauding are essential to our understanding of self and sexuality. I also want to offer healing for the roots of our victimization, those things in our past that imprinted the pattern wrong. To benefit maximally, you will need to be rigorously honest—honest about what others have done to you as well as what you have done to yourself and others.

Seduction

Seduce: To attract, charm, lure, or entice.

Seduction in a relationship is manipulation that is calculated to gain attention, affection, or something else to meet a need. It can be done consciously or unconsciously and be subtle or overt, mild or strong.

*This vicious cycle
of victim and victimizer
is a hard one to face.
Nobody wants to see
themselves as a victimizer
(perpetrator) of others.
It is much easier to see
ourselves as the victim
of someone else's
actions than face our
own contribution.*

There are also different motives behind seduction. Sex, surprisingly, is one of the lesser ones.

Our entire culture is based on seductivity. So much so that we take it for granted, not realizing its harmful effects in our lives. TV commercials are designed to charm, allure, or entice us into buying their products. Billboards do the same. Each is a manipulation calculated to attract our attention. It has become so common that we now believe in seduction. We accept it as a tool for everything from buying cars to establishing a relationship.

Take dating, for example. Each person is focused on accentuating strengths and hiding weaknesses in order to attract the other person. But there are inherent dangers in this approach.

Scripture warns women not to place too much emphasis on the outer adorning of their body, but rather to concentrate on inner qualities of beauty (see 1 Peter 3:3–4). This principle has much to say to men as well. Why? Well, when women or men concentrate more on external qualities than internal, they will jeopardize character development and become seductive in their relationships. They will tend to attract others and keep them through use of their looks rather than their character, which can lead to shallow relationships and a focus on sexual activity without emotional depth.

And, sadly, concentrating on outer qualities at the expense of transparency, trust, integrity, and honesty will only yield unfulfilling sex.

Victimized Women

If I have heard the statement once, I have heard it a thousand times. It seems to be every wife's chief complaint: "I wish he would pay more attention to me instead of watching sports all the time." This is commonly followed by, "The only time he shows any interest in me is when he wants sex."

Sadly, the complaint is very true of marriages today. Many men are not responsive to their wives' needs. Even more tragic is that a woman may end up divorcing one inattentive spouse just to end up marrying another, all the while wondering what went wrong.

A woman in this situation is often not in touch with how her own seductiveness is causing her to be victimized. She is, in effect, victimizing herself.

When a woman dresses, acts, and does everything she can to attract the attention of a man, she is appealing to his sensual nature. In focusing on enticing men through her looks, she will always attract the kind of man who is more drawn to looks than to character. She will have unwittingly appealed to his baser instincts, and he will give her the response her seductivity calls for because he will want what the seductivity promises. This sets up the foundation for him to give her love to get sex.

Later in the relationship, she will feel defrauded because he only gives her love when he wants sex. Characteristically, she will complain and feel victimized by him, not realizing that she has contributed to the victimization through her own seductivity. Seductivity always attracts what you eventually do not want. It leads to a pattern of codependent sex.

Characteristics of Seductiveness

I want to offer a number of characteristics that usually indicate seductivity in a woman. But first, let me caution you on one very important thing: Seductivity is a manipulation calculated to fulfill an inner need. It has more than one facet to its expression. The "floozy" with the bulging breasts and skin-tight pants is an extreme example of seductivity—there are many levels in between. One does not have to fit every trait to be considered seductive; but if many of them apply, then it is a major facet of your life. A revealing exercise might be to have others evaluate you.

1. She draws the attention of men to herself, even though at times she may feel awkward with that attention.
2. She will want to catch a man but not always want to live with one.
3. She is preoccupied with physical appearance, meaning one or more of the following:
   - she is body conscious
   - really into clothes—a "clothes horse"
   - dresses to accentuate her breasts, buttocks, or waist
   - always has to be stylishly dressed
   - worries about gaining weight
   - sacrifices health for beauty
   - spends a lot of time on her appearance
4. She dresses for men, often in competition with other women.
5. She can't be happy without a man in her life.
6. She does not enjoy the company of women as much as men.
7. She feels insecure around beautiful or seductive women.
8. She falls for men who:
   - give her attention
   - make life exciting for her
   - need her
   - look good to other women

9. She gives men a lot of power over her life by always needing their approval or acceptance.
10. She has a history of repeat performance with inadequate or irresponsible men.

If a number of the above-listed traits resemble you, then seductivity is an issue in your life. You have bought into the false notion that you have to entice a man to love you. You may end up believing that it is your attractiveness that is responsible for making the relationship work, or that his inattentiveness is totally to blame for it not working. Either position is a setup for codependency, giving too much for all the wrong reasons. It is also a setup for codependent sex, which may eventually lead to a waning of your desires, resulting in inhibited sexual desire.

The resolution to seductivity requires the following. If diligently embraced, change will come.

1. *Admit to your seductivity*. Recognition and ownership are always the first step to change. Many women do not want to admit to seductivity because they fear it puts them in the same league as a blatant seductress. But you don't need to be embarrassed about your weakness. Being seductive does not have to mean that you are a "floozy," but rather that your pattern of meeting inner emotional needs is self-defeating. If you allow embarrassment or shame to keep you from honest admission, then you will not become free. Also, remember that you cannot change your partner but you can change yourself.

2. *Look beneath your seductive behaviors to the needs you are trying to get filled by being seductive.* The roots of seductivity always lie in unmet needs

from the past and low self-esteem. These needs for love, acceptance, attention, affection, belonging, or appreciation are what fuels the lacking self-worth, hence the seductivity and codependency.

In the next section, I have described the typical roots of seduction, roots that come from our childhood. Carefully and prayerfully examine each. They may offer the key to freedom.

Roots of Seduction and Victimization in Women

Seductivity comes from the ways in which you as a woman have been consciously or unconsciously victimized by others. This especially means your parents. Most parents are very responsive and caring, but they are not perfect. Because parents have problems in life that detract from their ability to parent well, families will always be less than perfect and sometimes even dysfunctional. The natural extension of this is that kids will have a less than perfect, sometimes hurtful, legacy to contend with in adult years. Examining these root deficiencies is not an invitation to blame but rather an attempt to clear up the foundations and lay new healthy ones.

If tears or fears come, do not run from them. Take your time and ask Jesus to help you through the pain. It may help to examine these roots with a trusted friend or counselor. Writing out what you experienced can also be helpful.

1. *Dad was emotionally or physically absent.* When a father does not bond closely to his daughter, the lack will cause legitimate needs for approval, attention, or affection to go unfilled. The daughter may then try to get the needs met through other men.

2. *Dad was enmeshed or bonded too closely with his daughter.* If the bond is too close, one of partnering rather than parenting, then the adult daughter will feel unfilled if some other man does not intimately fill dad's place in her life. She does not know how to be complete in herself.

3. *Dad encouraged and reinforced the seductivity.* If dad was concupiscent—overly focused on sex—then he may have paid too much unhealthy attention to his daughter's emerging femininity. He may have given her attention only for her sexual and seductive behaviors, which laid the foundation for her to respond in these ways to get other men's attention.

4. *The parents were immature.* The needs of the child conflicted with the needs of the parents and lost. The parents were not nurturing and disciplined, but inattentive, neglectful, angry, rejecting, fearful, or overprotective. The daughter's needs for love, affection, and attention were not seen or met.

5. *Mom was seductive.* The daughter imprinted from mom because she was closely bonded to her. She picked up mom's behaviors, mom's style of getting needs met. She imitated the only thing she knew.

6. *There was favoritism in the family.* The family as a whole, or especially dad, prized sons more than daughters. Perhaps a son was wanted when she was born. Or maybe others in the family were prized by mom and dad more than she was. In any combination, the favoritism will create a need to win approval and attention from a man in order to validate her worth.

7. *There was a devaluing of women.* It wasn't simply that men were shown favor, but women were not prized or valued in her home. Maybe they were seen as only having value through how they might please and serve a man. Or there may have been wrong judgments about maleness and femaleness, such as boys are smarter, girls are nicer, boys get praised for accomplishments, girls for beauty. The devaluing will cause her to perform for men in order to gain their approval.

8. *She was physically or sexually abused.* The wound of the abuse will have caused deep feelings of inadequacy, shame, and confusion. Deep within she will not feel good about herself. She will need men to like her and value her so that she can value herself.

9. *She was made to feel bad, wrong, or unacceptable.* Through whatever means, she grew up feeling "less than." The deep feelings of inadequacy, shame, and low self-worth will cause her to want men to approve of her so that she can feel good about herself.

There are so many other roots to seductivity that no listing could describe each one. These, however, are among the most common. If any of them remind you of you, then explore them in detail by finding out:

- what happened,
- how you felt about what happened,
- what inner judgments were made about what happened,
- what inner promises, if any, were made, and
- what need was unmet by what happened that is now fueling the seductive pattern.

Knowing these can lead you to a place of reeval-uating the events, recanting the self-defeating vows, forgiving the offenses, releasing the feelings, and surrendering the unfilled needs to Jesus. Only he can supply all your needs. If you try to fill deep, untapped needs for love, attention, and affection by yourself, through others, then you run the risk of seductivity and self-victimization. Surrendering them to him and finding healthy paths to fulfillment will bring true peace and help you avoid the trap of victimization.

Seduction in Men

Men are also seductive. Their style of seductivity parallels a woman's, only they are into clothes, body-building, and good-looking cars. All are calculated at-tempts to entice women and get their attention. But their seductivity goes beyond that. Studies have shown that women are more affected by what they hear and feel rather than by what they see. So I am sure this fact is what is behind the proverbial "line" each guy lays on a gal after he gets her attention.

But why do men want the attention of women, and what do they do with it? I believe the dynamics of a man's seductiveness are different from a woman's. A woman desires the validation a man gives her through his willingness to pursue and attend her. She needs his direct attention to feel affirmed, so much so that she will give him sex to get it. She wants him to look at her, talk to her, and tell her how special she is. The words mean everything.

Men, however, are different. The words count but the actions count more. A study revealed that men rarely believe what women tell them. They perceive women's words as fickle and untrustworthy. Women's actions, on the other hand, were very important. The greatest act of perceived trust was the willingness of a woman to surrender herself sexually to the man. This may be the key relational difference between men and women. *Men want a woman's validation through her sexual surrender to them. Women want a man's validation through his attentiveness to her.* Maybe this is why men give attention to get sex and women give sex to get attention.

The Scriptures warn men not to possess their wives in the "lust of concupiscence" but rather in "honor and sanctification." I believe this admonition reflects what is wrong with most men's sexual practices. Men desire to possess women in order to fulfill their sexual and emotional needs. Now, the need to possess is not the problem. Men are anatomically suited to possessing a woman sexually. A woman's surrender is also powerfully enriching. However, many, if not most, do it in concupiscent ways that dishonor women. By that I mean ways that reflect a lustful rather than loving expression of sex. Sex for human beings is not and should not be only a physical act of pleasure. Unless the law of love rules sex by seeking the best for the beloved, it will violate boundaries and ultimately doom fulfillment. It will make sex hurtful.

The Scripture also says that men have to "learn" how to do this. Sex for humans is not something that "just comes natural." It is a symphony of choreographed expressions, all attuned to the two involved individuals. Men must learn how to balance their desires with their partners' desires, or else they will victimize the women as well as themselves.

When the desire to possess is not rightly managed, it violates the other person's boundaries. And when boundaries are violated, the other person restricts access—meaning he/she will either withhold sex or withhold full emotional surrender during sex. The man will sense the inhibition, frequently redoubling his efforts to possess. Then, when the desire to possess is redoubled or strengthened, it will fuel a tendency toward compulsive or addictive sex. Such sexual practice further violates and further frustrates the man. He will not see how his pattern of concupiscence is contributing to his own victimization.

Healing Victimization and Defrauding in Men

Ryan's compulsive need for sex was begun by the wounds he experienced growing up. His mom sensualized him, and his first girlfriend surrendered to another. Both incidents "defrauded" him. *When sexual possession is thwarted, defrauding is the result.* The man feels cheated out of the sex he desires. This feeling of being cheated empowers a greater desire to possess that which was withheld. And when pornography or masturbation is added to the equation, it fuels the desire and sets him up for further feelings of being defrauded when a woman does not surrender to the measure his desire demands.

Healing for victimization or defrauding in men and its resultant sexual compulsion requires honest evaluation in four areas.

1. *Bring to recollection the times you felt defrauded.* These may include incidents where you were not entitled to sex with the person, but you still felt defrauded. Focus especially upon first memories with mom, sisters, and girlfriends. A woman who exposed part of her nakedness to you in a way that stirred your desire can also be a defrauding. Include women who

have teased you with their sensuality or seductivity. Also include times when you were allowed to touch and feel but not release.

2. *Try to get in touch with how these incidents made you feel.* Were you hurt, embarrassed, angry, or afraid? Healing requires experiencing the feelings. If you have difficulty identifying feelings, get someone to help you. If you talk about these issues out loud with a competent friend or counselor, the feelings will come in time.

3. *Examine how you have added to the defrauding by pornography, masturbation, or other means.* Have you fantasized, nursing and rehearsing your desire to possess? Or have you peeked in windows, looked up women's skirts, or always tried to see through the buttons of their blouses? It will have dramatically fueled your concupiscence.

4. *Go to Jesus. Ask him to heal the emotional imprint and pain of defrauding.* Forgive those who have defrauded you, whether they did so knowingly or unknowingly. Also ask forgiveness for the ways in which you have added to the problem. Offer him the wounds that have come from your own victimization of self, asking for a healing of the concupiscence and a restoring to innocence.

The roots of seduction, victimization, and defrauding are deep. They are wounds from the past, stored as hurtful memories. Let me refer you again to the chapter "Healing the Memories That Hurt"; it will also help.

Victims will victimize others and themselves if not healed. Perpetrators will do the same. Both have been victimized by the unhealed wounds of their past and the ways in which each have contributed to their own problem. Restoration to innocence comes with the willingness to honestly face one's self and God.

Chapter 7

TRACING SURFACE PROBLEMS TO ROOT SOLUTIONS

There are many paths to healing. What may work for one individual does not necessarily work for another. It obviously depends upon the uniqueness of the person and the problem. Even two individuals with the same problem may experience a different degree of struggle. Problems have differing strengths, and we all have varying abilities.

But no matter what your sexual difficulty, the paths to healing must cross over the same landscape. The common saying, "God's methods are many, His principles few; the methods may vary, the principles never do," is especially true in resolving sexual issues. The principles of change do not change. There are certain root issues that contribute to all sexual difficulties, whether you are inhibited, addicted, or abused. Whether your problem is powerful or slight. There are also specific things one must do to be healed. As we've said before, recognition and ownership of the problem are always the first step to healing.

Recognition and Ownership

Recognition is the open admission that there is a problem. Ownership is the personal affirmation that the problem I see is mine. To begin the process of healing, people must recognize what the problem is and also admit to the fact of the problem being their own, not someone else's. This not only puts the responsibility for change where it belongs, it further creates the hope for change because we can only change something that is ours to change. Witness the countless number of husbands and wives who have tried unsuccessfully to change their mates. We can, however, take responsibility for change in our own lives.

But the going won't be easy; eventually, we'll run up against that great enemy of change: denial. Denial is the tendency in all of us to avoid the truth about ourselves or others because it might hurt. Denial may soothe our senses for a while, but it can keep us in bondage forever if we let it. The truth does hurt, but it will set us free because we'll be able to honestly face the problem and change it. Rest assured, openly admitting to a problem is half the battle. But it is hard, if not impossible, to heal something that does not exist! It takes great courage to face one's deficiencies.

Courage

Courage is endurance in the presence of fear. I have been terribly afraid to look at myself and face my weaknesses, fearful that if others knew they would not approve of me. Greater yet has been my fear that if I really knew, how could I approve of myself? But I have learned a truth about myself and others: I will never be at peace with life, God, or myself until I face my own humanity and fear it no longer. Admitting that I am weak and deficient has removed the sting of my shame. And offering my insufficiency to God has invited his strength and sufficiency to do for me what I could not do for myself.

Sexually wounded individuals must courageously face their deficiencies and fears, especially if others have contributed to the deficiency or have their own problem. The tendency is always to take the speck out of our brother's eye without plucking the beam from our own (see Luke 6:41–42). Or to be so fearful of our own beam that we avoid doing anything. Both positions reflect important attitudes of heart that must be examined.

Attitudes of Heart

Woody Allen, in one of his movies, was pictured telling his psychiatrist that he and his wife only had sex once or twice a week. In the next scene, his wife was shown talking to her therapist, declaring that they had sex at least three or four times a week. Obviously, they both had sex with each other the same number of times, but each carried a different perception of the truth. The difference was related to their inner attitudes regarding sex. Woody prized sex greatly and wanted more. He was minimizing their actual experience. She wanted less sex and was maximizing.

At the very core of all sexual practice is a collection of deep inner beliefs about sex, self, and others. Associated with those beliefs are feelings and thoughts. Thoughts can trigger the feelings and feelings, in turn, produce more thoughts. All combine to reflect one's deep inner attitude of heart. This is why

At the very core
of all sexual practice
is a collection of deep
inner beliefs about sex,
self, and others. This
truth reflects the
difficulty with most
solutions to sexual
problems—they are
surface solutions
lacking the power
to change one's
inner attitude
of heart.

the author of Proverbs says, *"Above all else, guard your affections. For they influence everything else in your life"* (Prov. 4:23 TLB).

A change of sexual practice normally requires a change of heart.

Our genetics, families, and early relational and sexual experiences all come together in creating our innermost attitudes toward sex, self, and others. Sexual expression becomes a complex collection of thoughts, feelings, and behaviors all emanating from our core beliefs.

This truth reflects the difficulty with most solutions to sexual problems—they are surface solutions lacking the power to change one's inner attitude of heart.

Changing Attitudes

To most effectively change an inner attitude, two processes must occur simultaneously. Positive, clear, truthful messages must be input while negative contributing factors are eliminated. This boils down to re-education and healing. *The truth about sex, sexuality, and one's self needs to be embraced while old hurts, memories, and untruthful messages are removed.* The illustration below shows how attitudes are formed and changed.

Positive		Negative
"I LIKE"		"I DON'T LIKE"
"I WANT"		"I DON'T WANT"
"I CAN"		"I CAN'T"

Each bucket becomes filled with experiences, thoughts, and feelings that tilt us either positively or negatively. If the positive bucket is full, and the negative only partially full, then one's attitude will tilt toward the positive—"I like," "I want," or "I can."

If the negative bucket contains many hurtful experiences, thoughts, and feelings, with few positive ones in the other bucket, then the resultant attitude will be negative—"I don't like," "I don't want," "I can't."

Positive sexual attitudes motivate us to anticipate and enjoy sex. Negative ones cause inhibition, disinterest, or perversion.

Attitudes can be formed by repeated similar experiences. Recurring negative sexual experiences begin to reinforce a budding negative attitude toward sex, eventually creating an aversion toward sexual activity and encouraging inhibition.

But repeated positive experiences can also effect attitudes. This is the principle behind encouraging couples with sexual conflict to start with pleasuring exercises. It reduces the tension, restores intimacy, and builds confidence. Confidence is a positive "I can" attitude.

Prayer before sex can also be a major enhancement. Not only does prayer invoke divine intervention, but it usually puts our attitude in right order. Repeated healthy messages about sex and positive sexual experiences will form healthy sexual attitudes.

Attitudes can also be developed through powerful singular events, as if a huge rock was dropped in one of your attitude buckets. A single traumatic event can have the power of many smaller experiences.

Traumatic Events

Childhood sexual molestation or incest is usually a huge rock in one's negative bucket. Sex can powerfully affect a small child. When such private territory as sexual parts is invaded, lasting messages are imprinted deep within the child. Rape is another especially violating event. The more the event violates one's boundaries, the larger the potential of a negative attitude.

Early hurtful sexual experiences or molestations are at the root of many people's sexual difficulties, because as a small child we did not have the wherewithal to properly evaluate and resolve the experience. The resulting attitudes and core beliefs formed from these traumatic events were negative and unhealthy, and the positive bucket was just not full enough to compensate or balance out the negative.

When negative experiences are resolved or healed, however, the effect is one of removing the experience from the negative bucket and even placing it in the positive. But the problem with most childhood molestations, incests, or abuses is that children rarely have the knowledgeable support available to them to resolve the wound. Most perpetrators of abuse have already scared or shamed children into not telling. And tragically, sometimes when the children do tell, they are often discounted or shamed more. Even if the parents do listen, they are not usually equipped to walk the child through the necessary issues of resolve. A gifted counselor can help immeasurably. But make sure the counselor knows how God heals abuse and how he does it in kids.

Judgments and Vows

The repeated experiences and traumatic events of our life shape us by forming our inner attitudes. But one word of caution. *It is not just what happens to you that affects you but what you say to yourself about what happens.*

How we judge the experience is crucial. What we evaluate as right or wrong, good or bad lays the foundation of our attitude. Equally important is how we feel about the event. Painful events cause us to make inner pledges or vows to ourselves that commit us to act only in specific ways because of what we have experienced.

Ryan vowed never to let another woman reject him as his high school sweetheart had and never again to be cheated out of the sex he felt was due him. The result was a pattern of giving women love to get sex, then withdrawing before they could hurt him. His unhealed wound set in motion powerful self-defeating vows that resulted in negative attitudes and hurtful practices against women.

Vows and judgments are the building blocks of attitude. They heavily weight the bucket . . . usually in a negative direction. By identifying and supplanting unhealthy, negative judgments, you can greatly empower a change of attitude. Ryan came to see how he had judged all women as unfaithful based upon his experiences. He further realized he had also judged himself as sexually undesirable. This inner evaluation pressured him to push for sex in order to prove his desirability. Negative judgments about ourselves or others never help—they merely hinder us and lead us to form new vows.

Change of attitude is also empowered by isolating and recanting the unhealthy vows we make to ourselves. Ryan's vows got him into trouble and did nothing to heal his wounds of rejection. In fact, sexual obsession or inhibition is often empowered by inner pledges of protection made during times of wounding. These need to be uncovered and released. Listening to one's self-talk can help reveal and change the judgments and vows.

Self-talk

The constant inner conversation we have with ourselves about ourselves and the world around us is called *self-talk*. It is the inner voice that evaluates our experiences and reflects our inner attitudes. If you were to stop reading and listen to yourself think, you would be hearing your self-talk. Self-talk controls your inner response to outer events, forms the judgments and registers the vows we all make, and is the vehicle we use to establish inner attitudes.

If you think something over and over again in your mind, it is like adding stones to your bucket. The more frequently you think the thought, the more stones you add and the more your attitude develops in the direction of your thought. For example, nursing and rehearsing an old resentment will build a powerfully negative attitude toward the person who offended you. In contrast, remembering over and over again a special event will put rocks in your positive bucket and build a positive attitude toward the event and what it represents.

One writer has stated that over a million thoughts a day go through our minds. This makes what you worry or think about in a day's time very significant in forming or reinforcing attitudes.

Self-talk not only forms attitudes but reflects existing controlling attitudes. "For as he thinks in his heart, so is he" is a true proverb (see Prov. 23:7). What your self-talk says reflects your true beliefs. Changing one's sexual practices requires knowledge of the underlying core beliefs we are operating from. Knowing your inner thoughts about sex can help you identify your true beliefs. Being able to "listen in" to your self-talk can yield valuable insights into what needs changing and lead you to the discovery of the empowering inner vows.

Journaling

Most people have a notion of how they feel, but they lack clear knowledge of in-depth thinking and feeling. Journaling is a good technique to help discover hidden judgments and vows. If you've never journaled before and you don't know what to write, start out by recording what you're thinking about before, during, and after sex. One word of advice, though—the journal in which you write needs to remain private; it needs to be a safe place where you can record what you're truly feeling and thinking.

Since our lives tend to follow streams of thought over a number of days, I would recommend writing in your journal every day. This way, the pattern of thoughts and feelings that influence your sexual practices will soon become clear, which is why journaling is such a valuable tool for change. Negative inner thoughts need to be uncovered and controlled to assure healthy living. By controlling your self-talk in a way that affirms God's perspective of sex and sexuality, you will have taken your first step in beginning the change process. Your journaling will have isolated the key thoughts you need to resist, and after isolating them, you can then prayerfully ask God to give you a truthful Scripture verse or statement to replace your negative thought. Once you have that verse, write it down next to the negative thought and recite them aloud together, over and over again. Soon the truthful one will overshadow the other, thus leading to a change of attitude.

Light really does overcome darkness, and God's truth will win over falsehood.

A Standard Is Essential

The Scriptures, Judaism, and most Christian religions have taught that sex is God's gift . . . that it is to be sacred and pleasurable. Society, however, has maintained the pleasurable value of sex but has refuted the notion of its sacredness. To be sacred means to be dedicated to a singular purpose or person, thus worthy of reverence or respect. In today's society, though, there are seemingly few boundaries to sexual expression.

Since most people have exchanged traditional do's and don'ts for more permissive guidelines, their standards of practice are based upon what feels good or seems right at the moment. This has fostered trivial, banal, and promiscuous sex—sacrificing long-term gain for short-term pleasure. If we want sex to remain healthy and pleasurable, however, standards must be established and boundaries honored. Respect for something has everything to do with the boundaries one establishes to protect and preserve it. When boundaries are absent, sex becomes unhealthy.

Boundaries

Personal boundaries are protective devices. When honored, they keep us from hurt. Like property fences, they help us establish where we end and others begin letting others know that they can go only so far and no further or they are violating. By the same token, they may be let down or have gates by which another can enter, but only by mutual permission. Due to the intensely private, vulnerable, and intimate nature of sex, boundary violations are especially wounding.

Types of Boundary Wounds

Sexual intimacy is a mutual invitation to lower the boundaries, open the gates, and allow access to each other's most intimate and private property. But even when allowed access to one's property, there are still gates to open, paths to follow, and doors to knock on. Sexual wounds come from ignoring the fence or not following the paths or not knocking on the doors.

If you have been abused, sexually neglected, cheated on, rejected, made fun of, touched unwillingly, harassed, shamed, been the victim of incest, molested, pressured, or threatened, then your boundaries have been violated.

You may, however, be inadvertently wounding yourself by having your boundaries too rigid. Individuals with inhibited sexual desire are often too protective of their inner being, wounding themselves by inviting others onto their property but having so many rules that it's too difficult for anyone to be or remain intimate. This victimizes the other person who thought your offer of sex could be actualized without such difficulty. Victims of sexual abuse frequently have low boundaries because the abuse kept healthy boundaries from forming. But they also have very narrow paths and locked doors, a result of the damage that keeps a person from being able to trust and respond sexually. The victimized person defrauds others by offering sexual intimacy that they are unable to truly provide.

You may also wound yourself by unwisely giving someone permission to cross onto your property and not adhere to the paths or knock on the doors. Codependents do this frequently. In order to get love, care, or attention, they invite others to jump over the fence and wreak havoc in their yard and home. Later they regret that decision. Sally blamed herself over and over again for being "so stupid." To get love, she promised her husbands anything they wanted. In giving so much, she was too permissive. Her message to them was "there are no paths, no doors, and no locks . . . do whatever you want." And they did. They did not respect her, often cheating on her with others or performing shameful sex acts with her. Her second husband even infected her with a venereal disease. When reality set in, she condemned herself, but this only led to self-pity and inaction, not freedom. She had not yet seen the need for healing her own wound.

Codependents need to recognize that even though by not protecting their boundaries they have wounded themselves, God still offers healing. They also need to face the person who has wounded them. Even though they gave the other carte blanche, a caring and considerate person would not have taken advantage of the offer. The other person needs to take responsibility for personal actions.

Additionally, you may wound yourself by wounding another. Not having honored someone else's boundaries can bring the wound of a pained conscience. During my college years, I selfishly used two women. The memory of what I did was so painful that I pushed it to the back of my mind until events caused me to face my own sin. Healing from my guilt required taking full responsibility for what I did to them. It required humility and brokenness, but not groveling. Healing the shame begins with honestly admitting how truly sinful we all are and how the essence of grace is recognizing our profound insufficiency and God's amazing acceptance.

Healthy Guidelines

Healing and change require careful examination of your existing standards and boundaries for sexual expression. To begin this process, measure your sexual experience by the following guidelines. I believe they are all in keeping with a biblical perspective of healthy, fulfilling sex.

- Sex cannot be used to demean or physically abuse another person.
- Sex is unhealthy if it makes another person feel less than a valuable creation of God.
- Sex is unhealthy when it is selfish, used only for physical gratification and personal convenience.
- Sex is unhealthy when it shames another.
- Sex is unhealthy when the "law of love" does not rule.
- Sex is harmful when its practice hurts those involved or the ones they love.
- Sex is damaging when forced, pressured, or coerced.
- Sex is unhealthy when it is used as a substitute for affection, tenderness, caring, and intimacy.
- Sex is unhealthy when its practice violates one's conscience.
- Sex is harmful when practiced outside the confines of covenantal love (i.e., marriage).

Steps to Take

Depending upon one's background and willingness, the process of change could take years or just a short period of time. Either way, the signposts along the road must be heeded. The following steps will be helpful in walking through your problem or in helping other people with theirs.

1. *Have you faithfully tried pleasuring techniques?* Even when the cause of dysfunction is tied to the past, a pleasuring exercise aimed at correction can help. It will not work by itself all the time, but usually, when it's done in conjunction with the other steps to healing, the exercise can facilitate change. A word of caution—*Playboy,* XXX-rated movies, love potions, etc., are rarely helpful and can produce more problems than they solve. (See chapter 9, "Answers for Common Sexual Problems," for reference books that offer healthy pleasuring techniques.)

2. *Have you analyzed and overcome current relational issues and negative patterns that may be contributing to the sexual response problem?* Long-standing, unresolved conflicts are reflected in the sex act. The style of relationship both enjoy or endure in the front room will be carried into the bedroom. Sex creates relationship as well as reflects relationship. It will mirror both the positive and negative patterns. Most negative relationship problems began in the families we grew up in and have been carried into our marriages, where the pattern has become more established. Overcoming negative patterns requires three things: First, you must be aware of what healthy patterns of relationship are. This allows you to examine your existing ways of relating to see if they are unhealthy. Second, one must come to know how the pattern works, especially realizing your own contribution to the action-reaction pattern. Many negative patterns are created by someone else's wrongdoing and our unhealthy response to it. Third, you need to dis-

cover which relationship(s) in the past had a similar style or pattern of relating. Invariably, the pattern started with someone in your family or close circle of relationships. This is one reason why restoring innocence requires examining and overcoming negative family legacies. Once these three ingredients are evident, you will be able to deal with the roots from the past that are empowering the present.

3. *Have you looked in depth at your own beliefs about sex?* It is hard to develop a healthy view of sexuality in this overly sensual society. Sex is used too much to do too many things. But it is one's core beliefs about sex that controls practice. Your journaling should show you the judgments, vows, and beliefs you need to change. An excellent help in this area is Joseph Dillow's book *Solomon on Sex*, which provides a refreshing and insightful commentary on healthy sexual belief and practice.

4. *Carefully examine the roots of your life.* Your family and early sexual relational experiences have deeply affected you. Our families teach us our first lessons in sexuality, and our first experiences cement the pattern of response. Continue to explore the key family and relational roots that have contributed to your sexual development and difficulties.

5. *Face your wounded state.* Most of us have wounded ourselves or others and have also been wounded. Healing comes as we are willing to face the deep wounds of the past and offer them to God for healing. Do not be afraid of the pain. It will not make you crazy if you face it and face Jesus with it. The next

chapter, "Healing the Memories That Hurt," will take you step-by-step through your wounds to healing.

6. *Trust God, not just yourself or others.* Healing the wounds and conquering the powerful roots of abuse, obsession, or dysfunction require a power greater than us. Since God is the one who designed our sexual nature, he alone can deliver us from our self-defeating ways. So don't be afraid to take your request to him in prayer, because prayer is the primary requisite of change. God does everything through prayer and nothing without it. The more you pray and the more effectively you know how to pray, the greater the potential for change. In many of the chapters that follow, prayer steps are offered to help with more effective prayer. A note of special consideration: While dealing with these issues it helps to have a supportive friend or counselor who will pray for and with you. One person praying can send a thousand to flight, two can send ten thousand. The effectiveness of prayer is multiplied when others join us in seeking the healing and change we so desperately need.

Remember, Jesus is near the afflicted and wounded of spirit. "He heals the brokenhearted / And binds up their wounds" (Ps.147:3). And he sets the captive free (Luke 4:18).

Chapter 8

HEALING THE MEMORIES THAT HURT

*P*ost Traumatic Stress Disorder (PTSD) was a little-used psychiatric diagnosis until recently. Previously known as General Adaptation Syndrome, it has been commonly called combat fatigue or shell shock and was primarily restricted to diagnosing war veterans who had vivid recollections of their combat experience. Sometimes the trauma of combat leaves a haunting imprint that frequently lies dormant for years, surfacing later in dreams, flashbacks, or intrusive thoughts or feelings. War veterans can find themselves acting or feeling as if the traumatic event were recurring, especially when in contact with reminders of the event. They can also experience:

- Emotional shutdown, a numbing of feelings and a lack of responsiveness or interest in life.
- A startled response to sounds, touch, or even closeness.
- Sleep disturbance or fear of going to sleep.
- Unexplained guilt—from either having survived the trauma or over not having been able to prevent it.

- Memory impairment, an inability to remember parts of the past or the event, long gaps in memory, and frequent loss of time.
- Irritability or anger.
- Avoidance of any activity that resembled the trauma.
- Intensification of the symptoms when exposed to events that symbolized or resembled the trauma.

These symptoms are the body's way of signaling the veteran's desperate need to resolve the powerful impact of war and they'll continue until time and care are given to address that need.

This pattern of delayed stress response offers us insight into how any painful experience may affect us if not fully resolved at the time. Additionally, the post traumatic stress reaction establishes a protocol on how to deal with past unresolved wounds: We must face and relive the traumatic experience, processing the feelings, thoughts, and inner responses until the pain is gone.

Hurtful Wounds and Memories

All experiences of life are stored in the brain as memories, and unless the brain cells die or are damaged, these memories of life are recorded permanently. Not only is what we see, smell, touch, taste, and feel recorded, but how we evaluate events and what we vow to do as a result are also stored. Even though we may not remember, we still have the information stored within us.

Because people are sometimes too overwhelmed by an event to fully resolve their thoughts and feelings, they try to bury the pain and ignore the event, returning to normal as quickly as possible. But because that information is stored within us, doing so without resolution can wreak havoc in later life, causing it to surface again years later as a Post Traumatic Stress Disorder.

A similar pattern occurs with childhood wounds. Children do not possess the faculties to accurately and thoroughly deal with woundings, so they tend to dismiss what happened and go on. The unresolved wound, however, is stored as a hurtful memory begging for resolve. As time passes, the body will demand settlement of the issue. The outward symptoms may not be as severe as a Post Traumatic Stress Disorder, but they will be there. It all depends upon the severity of the trauma and the vulnerability of the individual.

Most of us need to revisit our childhood and family pasts to fully resolve the hurts that were never faced. Eve, Ryan, and others needed to face their hurtful pasts in order to break the power it had over their sexual practices and lives today. This is especially true for anyone who was molested or abused. If the abuse was severe or chronic, a full-blown pattern of Post Traumatic Stress Disorder can be evidenced in later life.

Sexual Abuse

Sexual abuse, rape, incest, molestations, and traumatic sexual and relational encounters can all be followed by a post traumatic stress reaction. Long after the event is over, the wounded person is still being affected by it. This was the case in Ann's life.

One Sunday during church, she had a fleeting picture pass through her mind of a small child being penetrated by a man's penis. She winced at the thought of such a thing, curiously feeling a tinge of pain herself. She dismissed the thought. A few weeks later she was humming a song and washing dishes. Again the picture returned, this time lasting longer. Ann immediately knew something was wrong. The picture was too familiar. Over the ensuing weeks, the realization came that she had been sexually molested by an uncle when she was about five or six years old. The memory of the abusive incidents had been blocked from her consciousness since childhood. But their influence was felt.

Ann was shut down sexually. When her husband, Ryan, touched her she would shiver and want to withdraw. And physically, it was painful. She had interpreted these symptoms as simply not liking sex as much as others. But with the return of the memories, she had to face the realization of her uncle's sexual abuse. This memory was especially painful because he had been one of her favorites. She also wondered why no one knew about it and why she had not told anyone. She did remember telling her mother that her vagina was hurting, but mom casually dismissed it.

Ann's exploration of her painful abuse led to many other questions and insights. Her uncle was an alcoholic who, in later years, was accused by a neighborhood girl of molestation. The family all sided with the uncle, saying the little girl had made it all up. Ann now knew better.

The return of painful memories, though difficult, also led Ann to healing. Her sexual practices and discomfort were tied to the abuse; she remembered, as a little girl, saying to herself that "sex hurts" and when she grew up she was not going to do it if she did not have to. She shed many tears, mourning the loss of her innocence, and she also recanted the vow she had made. And inviting Jesus into her memories to heal her pain brought comfort. Once her memories were healed, she was freed from the fear and pain, and sex became enjoyable. She still had steps to take, but now the path was clear of obstacles. Ann was being restored to innocence.

If she had resisted dealing with the memories or facing the pain, she could not have been healed. She would have continued in her pattern of codependent sex—giving sex only to get love and avoiding her husband's ire.

Caution

Do not ignore your fleeting memories or impressions or those of others. They may be true. If you are wondering whether or not you have been abused, talk about it. Getting it out in the open helps to clarify whether or not your memory or impressions are accurate. A competent Christian professional or a trained pastor can help you examine the evidence and confirm the truth. Also pray about it. Ask Jesus to show you the truth. It will come if you ask for it.

If painful memories begin to surface as you read this chapter, do not panic and run from them. Healing comes only as you face each one. But face them with Jesus and a trusted friend or counselor who knows how God heals sexual wounds and hurtful memories. If too many surface or they are too powerful, STOP. Resume when you are able. Take your time and make sure you have someone to help. But do not give up and run away. Jesus will heal you if you let him.

Other Factors in Abuse

Most incidents of sexual abuse occur with children who are too young to fully comprehend the trauma and know how to deal with the abuse. The perpetrator will often threaten or bribe the child, inducing fear, confusion, and shame. The bewildered child does not know what to do. The family, if told, frequently does not know how to respond either.

The reaction of "significant others" to sexual abuse greatly influences its traumatic effect on the child. A friend of mine shared the story of her family's reaction to the discovery that she had been molested by an uncle. When her father found out, he and her older brothers went after the uncle, severely beating him and forcing him to apologize to her. Her family's reaction shamed her even more than the incident. It caused her to try to forget it as quickly as possible. When a woman who has been raped has a spouse who overreacts or is unsupportive, it can also make recovery more difficult. In many cases, rape victims are tempted to remain silent rather than risk excessive reactions from family members.

On the other extreme, many families create an environment where sexual matters cannot be discussed, so when a child experiences molestation or incest, the "no talk" rule becomes a "no tell" situation. If the child tells what happened, repercussion is feared, especially if the abuse was perpetrated by a family member or close friend. Mothers who do not believe a daughter's tale of abuse force the shame and trauma underground, possibly even fostering continued abuse. When the child suppresses the incident, it surfaces later in life as PTSD. During sex the adult child may experience detachment, emotional deadness, or shame. The unresolved pain of the abuse continues to be connected with sex and sexuality.

Adults who as children were abused at night while they slept may have difficulty going to sleep.

They are reliving their unresolved childhood fear but do not know it. Anything in the present that consciously or unconsciously reminds them of the hurtful past can elicit the post traumatic stress response.

Another important factor to keep in mind is that the identity of the person who initiates sexual abuse greatly influences the depth of the trauma for the victim. The closer and more emotionally bonded one is to an assailant, the more powerful the result. This is why incest is especially damaging. Because parents have a tremendous effect in a child's life, an incestuous parent will profoundly confuse a child as to what love is and is not. The emotions a child feels are so overwhelming that the result is often detachment and dissociation from the incestuous act in an attempt to escape the horrifying fear and confusion. Dissociation is the act of separating one's self emotionally from the experience by pretending it is not happening, fantasizing about something else during the act, or trying to separate one's consciousness from self—watching the act as if an observer.

Repeated or ritualistic sexual abuse or incest can produce Multiple Personality Disorder (MPD)—a disorder characterized by the existence within the person of two or more distinct personalities, each with its own relatively enduring pattern of perceiving, relating to, and thinking about the environment and self. To put it simply, an abused child attempts to escape an overwhelming reality by creating an alternate one, another "self," to deal with the pain. The mind has a unique way of disconnecting us from reality when facing it would be too painful.

Sexual abuse in early childhood or adult years needs in-depth examination and healing. Memories need to be faced and their power broken. Survivors must realize how past events affect present circumstances in order to sever unhealthy ties. Facing painful memories is a necessary exercise. Not doing so perpetuates their control.

Other Reactions

Victims of abuse can experience a stress reaction that is not delayed. For some, the attempt to forget will be unsuccessful, as the pain and memory refuse to go away. When this happens, the body's natural tendency to forget is replaced by obsession. The thoughts are consuming and tormenting, and peace is nonexistent. I vividly remember the agonizing pain and shock of a woman whose husband had unexpectedly left her after thirty years of marriage. He had another family in another city and had been living a double life.

She absolutely could not believe it. She was unable to sleep, became emotionally numb, and began forgetting where she put things. The words of his good-bye note cycled over and over again in her mind. She felt guilty, thinking, "If only I had done something different, he would not have left." She was experiencing an acute traumatic stress reaction. The memories were powerfully in control of her life.

Jilted lovers, victims of unfaithfulness, and other wounded or abused persons can experience this kind of reaction where the memories do not easily go away. They also need healing of the hurtful memories so that peace will return.

If the wounded nurse and rehearse the events, they may become bitter. Many months later, Joe was bitter and preoccupied with the memory of catching his best friend and his girl having sex. He swore continually to get even and rehearsed in his mind how he would do it. This kind of behavior strengthens judgments and vows, empowering the hurtful memory even more. Unless there is a healing of the memory, it will indelibly imprint Joe in all the wrong ways. He will be tempted to give love only to get sex in order to get even. He will do this to help assuage his feeling of being defrauded. Or he may become codependent with someone who gives him the sex he feels cheated out of. His response will depend upon what he says to himself deep within. Either way, sex will not hold for him the healthy enjoyment he desires.

Healing the Memories

Unhealed memories are probably the single greatest cause of sexual dysfunction in women and men. The memories can come from any number of hurtful scenarios in or out of marriage:

- date rape
- rape
- sexual harassment
- molestation
- anal sex
- forced or pressured sex
- coarse jesting or teasing
- family attitudes
- angry sex
- shaming sex
- adulterous sex
- incest
- ritual sexual abuse
- sexual exposure by others or of self
- infidelity
- catching a sexually transmitted disease
- obscene phone calls
- inappropriate touch

The painful feelings associated with the memory need to be released. The memory of what was smelled, touched, or tasted will usually remain the same, but the negative emotions associated with the event can be changed. Additionally, our inner judgments and vows regarding the event must be re-examined and changed. They usually reflect our hurt, not our heart.

Healing the hurt requires facing personal wrong-doing as well as that of others. You must give yourself permission, and even the courage to remember what happened and how you reacted. The following steps have proven helpful to many in facing their wounds.

Invite the memories back. Do not be scared of old memories. If you are in a safe place with someone you trust, you can now handle what you could not handle then. Tears and feelings will come, but this time they can go and not have to come back.

Find a close friend or qualified Christian therapist to help. If the memories are many and the pain powerful, you will need both. A poem by T. Blake reads:

> I looked for my soul,
>> But my soul I could not see;
> I looked for my God,
>> But my God eluded me;
> I looked for a friend,
>> And then I found all three.

Many incest and ritually abused survivors owe their undying gratitude to friends and counselors who cared enough to walk with them through the memories, always supportive and prayerful. A therapist in our counseling center has done this for others, even at great sacrifice to herself and her family. God always provides those who will care, but you have to risk looking and asking for their help.

*Unhealed memories are
probably the single greatest
cause of sexual dysfunction
in women and men.
Re-examining your
wounded memories
can offer freedom from
the problems of today
that are empowered
by the past. Healing
the memories that hurt
helps restore innocence.*

Invite Jesus into the memory with you. You not only need others, you need him. He will provide you with the true perspective of what happened and what needs to be done. He will also provide the power for healing. Inviting Jesus into your memory may reveal your own hurt or anger with him for not protecting you. If this occurs, don't be afraid to tell him about it.

Tell him how you honestly feel. Healthy relationships require honesty. As I have shared my wounds honestly with Jesus, I have yet to be disappointed in the outcome. You can tell him anything and everything. He is not embarrassed or offended. Some say "Why tell? He already knows." Relationships are based on interaction and communication, not mind reading. Expressing yourself to him builds the relationship and gives him access to your deepest needs.

Look for the wrongdoing. Looking for the wrongdoing is necessary to release and resolve it. When facing hurtful memories and wounds, be careful to distinguish your own sin and wrong responses from others' sins and offenses against you. Do not make excuses for those who have wounded you or violated your desires. Reality must be embraced before healing will come. Also, do not excuse yourself. The pain of self-recrimination will leave as you accept your true responsibility and release it to God. It is okay to be wrong; no one is perfect. Ask Jesus to show you the wrong, and how he makes it right.

Examine your inner reaction to the event by discovering your judgments and isolating the vows. How did you evaluate the situation? Did you wrongly say it was your fault? Their fault? God's? What did you tell yourself about you? That you were too weak? Deserved it? Not good enough? Inadequate or inferior? Stupid? What did you say to yourself about sex? Dirty?

Bad? Distasteful? Shameful? Other inaccurate evaluations? What did you tell yourself about the other person? Members of the opposite sex? Were all your evaluations absolutely true or more the reflection of a wounded person or child?

If your evaluations were wrong in fact or even judgmental in attitude, you need to recant them and embrace the truth. The wrong evaluations are weighty stones in your bucket of negativity. You also need to isolate the pledges or promises you made to yourself as a result of what happened. Did you swear you would get even? Or that you would make sure no one ever hurt you again? As you isolate the vows and judgments, recant the unhealthy ones that have caused you and others pain.

Forgive yourself. Forgiveness is not pretending something did not happen. It is the full realization of the wrongdoing and a decision not to exact the penalty due. And forgiveness must be actualized before the pain is released. Ask God's forgiveness for what your judgments and vows have done to you and others. He always listens and responds. Especially when we take full responsibility for ourselves.

Forgive those who have wounded you. A pastor friend of mine once said, "All forgiveness is releasing the past." You will not be fully free of the past wound until you have forgiven those who hurt you. This doesn't mean that you have to place yourself in the same vulnerable position with the person again. On the contrary, if the other person has not truly changed and asked forgiveness, then exposing yourself to him or her again could be damaging. Sexual abuse victims in particular should be very cautious of resuming or maintaining relationship with the perpetrator, unless a formal process of reconciliation has been undertaken with the help of a counselor or member of the clergy. God can guide you as to whether you should or should not follow such a path, but you will rarely know if you should unless you have first forgiven. Forgiveness clears our eyesight by cleansing our motives.

If someone has hurt you so deeply that you feel you may never be able to forgive, then ask Jesus for his help. He understands. Be careful that you do not give yourself permission to remain bitter for long, because bitterness defiles you and those around you. If the bitterness will not go away, then pray, fast, and find someone to help you dig deeper into the bitterness. Something else may be empowering it. You need to discover the contributing factor before release will come.

Also, be careful that you do not forgive too soon. Quick and easy forgiveness says that the violation was minimal and the effect negligible. Make sure you fully realize how the other person has violated you, sinning not only against you but God. Make sure you are emotionally in touch with the depth of the offense. The feelings are an indication of really having dug into the bottom of the bucket. Christians, codependents, and "nice" people frequently do not look deep enough at the offense before forgiving, and that hinders the healing.

Ask Jesus to forgive you for your wrongdoing. There are two ways to sin against God. One is to commit a clear and unprovoked violation of God's law. The other is to react to someone else's violation in the wrong way. Either will cause you to stumble. To experience healing in this area, you will need to ask for forgiveness of the wrong ways you may have reacted to the other person's wrong. Did you become bitter? Vindictive? Seductive? Promiscuous? Your wrongdoing may be totally understandable given the circumstances, but it is still wrong. Admitting wrongdoing does not mean you are bad, only that you are now taking responsibility for something you were unable or unwilling to do then.

Look for the good in it. This may sound ludicrous to you, but every cloud does have a silver lining. To fully evaluate something requires an in-depth examination of both the detriment and value. Even abusive and hurtful experiences can yield positive benefits. Survivors of abuse, like prison camp survivors, frequently find their character strengthened from experience. The suffering may have given them an ability to endure seemingly unbearable circumstances, and those who have been wounded or who have suffered may be more sensitive to others and life. What has the experience done for you? If you are having difficulty seeing anything of value from your pain, ask Jesus to help you. You may also need more time and distance from the memory and pain before the positive can be seen.

Thank Jesus for his help and forgiveness. Believe he has heard you and realize something will change in you. Do not give in or give up. He does not.

This kind of memory work with prayer has led many to healing. When the wounds are healed, we can then set healthier boundaries for ourselves and others. We can embrace both the pleasure and sacredness of sex. Many of you will be able to trust again and be truly vulnerable in a healthy way for the first time. Reexamining your wounded memories can offer freedom from the problems of today that were empowered by the past. Healing the memories that hurt helps restore your innocence.

Chapter 9

ANSWERS FOR COMMON SEXUAL PROBLEMS

*I*t seems like most people we counsel or know have some type of sexual conflict, disappointment, or problem—usually someone wants sex more, less, or differently. That is why sexual problems fall into two general categories. The first is where the inability to fully embrace sexual functioning affects the person's life. The other is where the inability to stop or fully control sexual behavior affects his or her life.

The individual who has difficulty embracing all that sex could be may experience distinterest, pain, fear, aversion, or lack of orgasm. The ability to function sexually was damaged or never fully developed. These individuals usually practice codependent sex.

These who have difficulty with control had sex overemphasized or wrongly developed, which has led to obsession, compulsion, or deviation. They practice compulsive sex.

As we have seen in the previous chapters, our family backgrounds and past love experiences control our sexual fulfillment today. But our sexual problems are also fueled by the response each person makes to the perceived problem. If problems are ignored or denied, they fester and worsen . . . few problems go away on their own. But if they are confronted honestly and prayerfully, healing comes and change follows.

In this chapter, I have offered a brief description of the most common sexual problem areas, with insights for healing and change. Whatever your experience of sexual difficulty, it will probably fit one or more of the problem areas. For some, the problem may be powerful and overwhelming, while for others, it may have only nuisance value. For either, admitting to the problem and facing the issues can bring restoration.

Orgasmic Problems

"I can't have an orgasm like everybody else," was Mary's complaint. She and Paul had tried everything: vibrators, X-rated movies, the Kegel exercise, even *Playgirl*. At one time in their early years of marriage, they had even considered wife swapping. As Mary put it, "This has been a problem for me since our marriage first began. I don't like being this way, but I can't help it. I switch back and forth from being willing to try anything Paul says to not ever wanting to hear the word *orgasm* again!"

The lack of orgasm is a common complaint of many women. Most studies indicate that as many as half of all women are not routinely orgasmic. They may desire sex and enjoy it, even becoming aroused, but they often feel sexually inadequate or dysfunctional because it is hard for them to be orgasmic or multi-orgasmic like they read or hear they should. The heightened focus on female orgasm in recent

*Sexual problems fall into
two general categories.
The first is where the
inability to fully embrace
sexual functioning affects
the person's life. The other
is where the inability
to stop or fully control
sexual behavior affects
his or her life. Both need
insights for healing
and change.*

years has encouraged many to become orgasmic, but it has also made others more self-conscious and feel more unfulfilled. Self-conscious or disappointing sex is not good sex; the expectation of experiencing orgasm frequently becomes work rather than enjoyment. Paul and Mary had turned her lack of orgasm into a lifelong project—one that was ruining sex for her and keeping them both in the bondage of unfulfillment.

"Have you thought of letting go of your need for an orgasm?" I asked.

Mary quickly answered, "I would love to if Paul would let me. But he thinks we can't have good sex unless I have an orgasm."

"What about it Paul? Is Mary right?"

"I don't want to see her cheated out of what she could have. I think we just haven't tried hard enough. She never did those Kegel exercises for very long, and she also refused to really try and masturbate. I think if she would just try those two things everything would work."

Mary dissolved in tears. "Why do we always have to say that I just need to work harder on it and it will happen? I've tried and tried and tried and it hasn't worked. I am tired of trying and I'm tired of sex."

Hopeless silence filled the room. This was an old argument being rehashed and going nowhere—he wanting more effort and she wanting less pressure. Mary broke the silence.

"I'm sorry. I just got upset. I'll try again if you want me to."

"Mary, why are you willing to try again at something so painful?" I asked.

"Because it means so much to Paul. I don't want

to disappoint him anymore. I know it is hard to have a wife who isn't orgasmic."

"So the real reason you have tried so hard all these years is to please Paul, not yourself?"

"I don't care that much if I have an orgasm. I still enjoy sex, but it seems to mean an awful lot to him, so I've tried to have one so he would be happy."

"I think that's the problem. Orgasms can't be had for someone else. It has to be for you or it won't work."

Mary had become confused about her own sexual needs and responsibilities. She had never seen the need to fulfill her own sexuality through orgasm. For her, sex had only been a relational duty, not a personal fulfillment. She gave sex in order to get love. While it is admirable that she would care enough for Paul to try and please him, it was at the same time misplaced love. For sex to be truly healthy and fulfilling, it needs to be mutual. Only in rare circumstances will giving sex to please another and not also one's self be healthy and fulfilling.

Mary was quick to realize her error. Paul, however, was harder to deal with. At the root of the problem was his feeling of inadequacy if she did not have an orgasm. He was really wanting her orgasm for himself. He thought that if he were really a good lover, he should be able to make her or any woman reach orgasm. This is a common myth many men believe.

Now, there are things a man can do to help his wife—understanding, care, foreplay, and attention are but a few. A lack of pressure is another. But for many women, orgasmic response requires ownership, meaning the desire to experience an orgasm for themselves.

What are some of the things that influence a woman's orgasmic response? Early childhood experiences, births, proper foreplay, prior abuse, and being tired or distracted are just a few. For a large proportion of women, sexual response does not develop spontaneously as it does with men. It is more of a learned response that develops over time. First-love experiences, sexual beliefs, and parental influences also affect a woman's sexual development and orgasmic response. This means that the orgasmic response is wrapped up in the nuances of past and present relationships. Orgasmic dysfunction needs to be dealt with in terms of the imprint each of those relationships left.

Working toward an orgasm takes effort. Clifford and Joyce Penner, in their book *The Gift of Sex*, give specific pleasuring exercises a couple can use to develop sexual response. And Dr. Ed Wheat's book *Intended for Pleasure* also provides sound advice and exercises aimed at improving sexual and orgasmic response. His description of the how-to's and why's of the Kegel exercise is especially helpful.

How can you tell if you should continue to work toward an orgasm or not? Mainly by trial and error. Have your repeated attempts created pressure rather than progress, peace, and pleasure? Remember, sex is more than an orgasm. It is a ritual of feelings, touches, sensations, and involvement. It is meant to bring two caring, committed individuals closer and more deeply together. Orgasms are part of an overall sexual relationship of caring and commitment, but not the only part. Many nonorgasmic women can still have healthy, meaningful and fulfilling sex. As with many things in life, it is not just what you do that counts, but why you do it.

If you have faced these issues and followed through with the pleasuring exercises listed in the two recommended books and still do not experience orgasmic response, then you need to consider letting go of your pursuit. Orgasm may still be possible, but it cannot be your primary goal. Your focus may need to be directed toward the roots of your sexual development rather than behavioral change. Orgasm may come as healing is realized in those areas.

For Mary and Paul, sex had become a wedge in their relationship. Both, however, saw their need for change. It was difficult at first, but peace, pleasure, and fulfillment were restored. They set a new goal: to enjoy each other sexually. For them this meant less pressure with more gratitude and acceptance for what did work. It also freed Mary to focus on what she really needed to face . . . her past. She had unresolved relational issues with her family and a powerful secret. For four years from the age of ten, she had been the victim of incest with her half brother. Mary was ashamed of it, not even Paul had known. Dealing with her shameful secret would restore her innocence and might also release her to find orgasmic fulfillment.

Inhibited Sexual Desire or Excitement

Those who do not desire sex have what's called inhibited sexual desire. Others may desire sex, or at least not be adverse to sexual intimacy, but they have difficulty becoming aroused. This is what inhibited sexual excitement is. Either condition can be due to physical reasons, so an examination by a physician is often necessary to determine the cause. Usually, however, the cause is emotional rather than physical.

Inhibition has a lot to do with our family environment and the bonding patterns that began in childhood. If abuse is a part of our past, it will significantly contribute to a lack of desire or excitement.

Reading a book and eating were Pam's favorite pastimes—sex was not. Her husband insisted on counseling, hoping it would help their situation. When asked about sex, Pam responded, "I just never think of sex, and if I do, something inside says 'yuck.'"

As a child Pam had been neglected emotionally, spending many hours alone eating and reading. She had also been molested twice by a neighbor. Through these neglectful and abusive experiences, her sexual development had been arrested. To overcome her inhibited sexual desire, she needed to clear up the past and face her sexuality, which she'd been escaping through food and books.

By contrast, inhibited sexual excitement in women is expressed primarily as a lack of maintaining the vaginal swelling and lubrication during intercourse. The woman will either have difficulty becoming lubricated or will not be able to maintain lubrication. Somehow, her body does not respond excitedly to sexual contact. This condition can be due to such physical causes as a lack of hormones, but in most women, the root problem is sexual damage or inhibited development due to the unresolved hurts of past sexual experiences.

For women who do not desire sex or who have problems with excitement, it is much easier to ignore sex, hoping it will go away. But marriage is significantly improved with healthy sex. It was hard for Pam to face her own sexual needs as well as those of her husband, but it was necessary—and healthy. In her situation, her husband's pressure was helpful in breaking through the denial, because it would have been much easier for her to continue reading novels and overeating.

Healthy pressure can make us face our deficiencies and commit to doing what is necessary for change. Though the pressure may not always be easy to take, it is nevertheless healthy to struggle with ourselves and our limitations, it reminds us of our humanity. Pam needed to struggle with her self-indulgence and escapism, because she had never admitted to herself or others that she had a problem. The pressure brought truth.

Once a problem is recognized and ownership is taken, God gives the power for change. Mary needed to "let go and let God" take care of her orgasmic response. She had recognized the problem but now needed to surrender its resolve to God. Pam, on the other hand, needed to own having a problem before surrendering it to God for change. This is where wise counsel can help.

Impotence

In men, inhibited sexual excitement is often called impotence, which means that the man has trouble getting or maintaining an erection. In recent years, this has become a very common problem. Some authorities speculate that as many as one man in five may experience episodes of impotence during some period of his life.

Alcohol consumption, job stress, and being overweight are major contributors, along with such physical reasons as diabetes. But usually the root cause has to do with *resentment* and *resignation*. The resentment is usually aimed toward the wife, and resignation is usually directed at the idea that she and the problem are not going to change. Impotence can be his way of punishing her without having to deal openly with the conflict.

Besides resentment and resignation, impotence can also be a reaction to his own or his wife's expectations to perform. An occasional lack of erection is not unusual, especially as mid-life approaches. However, when anxiety or pressure develops over sexual performance, impotence can result.

Walter had difficulty getting aroused and also with maintaining an erection. The problem would usually come and go, but it was getting worse. His wife, Karen, complained bitterly about his lack of affection, attention, and sex. She also complained about everything else, especially the way he handled money. There was an obvious marriage problem. I referred Walter to a local physician to have an impotency test done. This is a test that measures whether or not a man has erections during the night. If he does, then one can safely conclude that his impotence is due to emotional factors, not physical. If, however, he does not have nocturnal erections, the problem is organic.

We called and set up the appointment for Walter, but he did not show. He also did not return for counseling for a few months . . . coming back only because of a new marital crisis. I asked him why he had not taken the test.

"I was too busy," he mumbled.

I pushed the issue. "Walter, I know it's more than being too busy. Tell me what you're really thinking and feeling."

He fumbled with his pen and stumbled over the words, "She embarrasses me."

Walter was a huge man, weighing close to three hundred pounds, with hands like baseball gloves. It was hard to picture this giant of a man embarrassed by his short, peppy wife.

"How does she embarrass you?"

"She says I don't do it right."

"She says you don't do sex right?"

"Yeah."

"What is it you do wrong?"

"Everything."

As we got more detailed, it was clear that Karen's critical nature was also being expressed in the bedroom. Walter could not do anything right. The harder he tried, the more he bumbled, and the more she criticized. It had become a vicious cycle.

He did not want to take the impotency test because he knew how the results would turn out, then he would have to face her and the truth that he did not want sex with her. Lovemaking had become too anxiety provoking for him. It was pain, not pleasure. Because he was only giving sex to get her off his back, his pattern of practice had become codependent.

What Walter and Karen needed was to have their marriage problems resolved. He was passive, she was aggressive, and both were out of order. As they dealt with their negative marriage pattern, sex improved. But the real breakthrough came when Walter was able to deal with his own shaming sexual past.

When he was a child, a male baby-sitter had molested him. He had totally forgotten about the experience until we began counseling and I had him do a personal sexual history.

After he had failed to show up for an appointment, I called. He answered the phone saying, "I can't come back and talk about those things!"

"Why not, Walter?" I asked.

"Because it's too embarrassing."

Once again the issue of embarrassment surfaced. I encouraged him by sharing my own past discomfort with sexual issues and how I had needed someone to trust. He agreed to return, and we were finally able to deal with the molestation and the shame it had created.

Childhood sexual abuse, molestation, incest, or even experimentation can breed shame that we carry into adulthood. Men and women with inhibited sexual desire or excitement need to look for roots of shame from their past which may be influencing them today.

Addiction and Sexual Problems

Impotence in men is frequently associated with alcoholism and certain drug addictions. The alcohol breaks down the man's male hormone, testosterone, causing impotence. Certain drugs also affect physical performance. Recovering alcoholics or addicts and their spouses need to be patient because it takes time to recover physically. There may also be relational problems in need of resolve and amends to be made before sex can work.

Promiscuity goes hand-in-hand with addiction, making guilt and shame big issues. Addiction may have caused some to violate others, commit adultery, indulge in shameful acts, or generally mismanage the gift of sex. Recovery from the addiction may require significant time and effort in dealing with the sexual past. Both the wounds inflicted on others and on themselves need healing before sex can be fulfilling.

On the other hand, some addicted individuals in recovery seem as if they cannot get enough sex. Their tendency is to substitute sexual comfort for the lack of alcohol or drugs. For them, abstinence or moderation will be difficult, since their deeper need is for the comfort only God can bring. If they continue to use people, sex, places, or things to try to meet that desperate inner need, they will remain addicted and powerless. God's Holy Spirit soothes the inner anxieties and brings peace to the inner being. Alcohol, drugs, or other substitutes only deaden the pain or give momentary pleasure.

Addicted individuals in recovery usually need their innocence restored, because when it isn't, it becomes a major factor in relapse.

Premature Ejaculation and Male Orgasm

These are two other conditions men experience as problem areas. Inhibited male orgasm is less common than premature ejaculation. In the first, a man may be excited and even maintain an erection but be unable to achieve orgasm. The lothario Don Juan was known to have difficulty with orgasm. Many men have secretly admired the ability to maintain an erection, not realizing that erections sustained for lengthy periods of time without orgasm can become painful, making sex unfulfilling.

This Don Juan image of being able to conquer women can be at the root of this problem. Too often, an inorgasmic condition represents unresolved inner attitudes of fear or resentment toward women. The man desires the woman's surrender but cannot return his. He cannot be vulnerable. This is why rape is more appropriately understood as an act of anger rather than lust. The rapist has a powerful need to conquer a woman, his sexual desires having become interwoven with his resentments and judgments against women as well as his unresolved feelings about his own masculinity.

The second problem, premature ejaculation, is

very common in men. It is the inability to control one's orgasm long enough to complete intercourse.

Bill commented to me during a session, "Every time I enter my wife, I immediately lose control and ejaculate." For many men, this pattern of quick release has been developed through pornography and masturbation while teenagers. The times of masturbation were quick and powerful, thus they trained themselves to quickly reach orgasm after arousal. This pattern becomes so ingrained that it persists into the marriage.

Some other causes of premature ejaculation are unresolved fear of or resentment toward women; performance anxiety, where the man is so afraid of disappointing or offending his wife that he gets sex over with as quickly as possible; or, for some, those who are married to inhibited women, the wife's unresponsiveness helps them into the pattern of quick sex and premature orgasm. Compulsive sexual practices can also lead to or reinforce premature ejaculation because the man is focusing too much on the orgasmic and sensual effects of lovemaking and not enough on the relational.

Regardless of motivation, premature ejaculation is tied to viewing women as objects of sexual gratification rather than intimate sharing partners. The too-quick release is his body's way of demonstating discomfort with lingering intimacy.

In an attempt to combat the premature ejaculation, many men try thinking about something that will turn them off. But this is unadvisable and even hurtful to sexual intimacy. A better solution is a technique called "squeeze control" that can be practiced by both partners together. If done faithfully, this will usually overcome the problem. Most couples who fail to overcome it are not putting enough time and effort into the technique to retrain the man's sexual response time.

Besides solving the problem, this technique has an added benefit. It builds intimacy. Through the man's admission of vulnerability and his wife's willingness to affirm and support him, walls of separation or discomfort are gradually torn down.

Painful Sex for Women

Pain or vaginal spasms during sex are two common problems for women. Because either condition can have a physical cause, such as a hormone deficiency or vaginal warts, a woman should seek a physician first before considering an emotional root cause.

When a physical cause has been ruled out, however, painful sex is called functional dyspareunia. This condition is frequently associated with pain from the past. The physical act of a grown man's penetration of a young incest victim causes pain. That pain continues in the memory and usually becomes associated with the act itself. Even though the memory of the abuse may fade, the memory of the pain does not.

This same phenomenon can create vaginal spasms, technically called functional vaginismus. The musculature of the outer third of the vagina involuntarily spasms during intercourse, also causing pain and discomfort.

This response is a graphic example of a woman's body rejecting the sex she says she wants.

Vaginal dilators, available from most doctor's offices, can help overcome the problem. However, there are usually emotional issues that need to be looked at as well. When we say one thing and our bodies say another, there is usually something we are not facing. These problems are signals to a woman from her body saying, "Look for the emotional pain sex represents." As the abuse or emotional stoppages of the past are faced and resolved, sex can indeed become fulfilling rather than fearful or painful.

Compulsive-Addictive Sex

Sexual compulsion is the acting out of sexual obsessions in repetitive, ritualistic, and uncontrollable ways. Ryan compulsively masturbated. No matter how hard he tried, he could not keep from doing it. He also pushed for sex even when he knew Ann was not interested. Before he left town on a trip he "had to have sex." When he returned home, he "needed it again." The sexually compulsive will risk rejection, pain, and even legal problems to act on their sexual impulses.

People can become sexually obsessed or compulsed through a wide variety of means: masturbation, pornography, X-rated movies, foot fetishes, sadomasochistic sex, prostitution, kinky sex. Sexually obsessed and compulsed individuals are best understood as sexual addicts. Rather than being in control of sex, sex is controlling them. Like a drug, sex is used to dull the pain, remove the shame, and bring comfort. When it does not work, addicts redouble their efforts to try again, thus creating a vicious cycle of temporary relief and continuing pain.

The roots of addictive behavior go deep into each person's childhood and first sexual experiences. These people are wounded . . . either by their own actions or by the actions of others. And unless change and healing come, they usually end up wounding others. For them sex has become frustrating, empty, or shaming; it is hurtful instead of helpful. They need the wounds healed in order to enjoy sex as God intended.

Hope

For all who struggle sexually, you know that hope is hard to find. Indifference, resentment, anger, and pain are all too often your frequent companions. But I have seen change in my life and countless others, so I can offer hope to you. The insights and steps provided can bring healing to your life if you will not give up and give in. Scripture says to "not grow weary while doing good, for in due season we shall reap if we do not lose heart" (Gal. 6:9). Overcoming sexual problems works the same way. If you do not grow weary in practicing those things that will bring wholeness, then in time, God will restore your innocence.

Chapter 10

CLEANING UP YOUR PAST: DO YOU REALLY HAVE TO TELL?

*T*here are differing opinions about whether or not to share one's sexual past with another, especially its indiscretions. I've never been quite sure what to advise others until I had to face my own past that unforgettable winter night. The air was cold and the fire inviting. After a long, hard day my brother remarked, "You know, Al, it was the strangest thing I had seen in a long time."

We were enjoying the ritual of ending a long day's hunt by swapping tales around the campfire at night. Gary, a firefighter, continued, "We answered a call on a wreck early in the morning, over by where you used to live. This guy was coming home from work, when he fell asleep at the wheel. He ran up over the curb into a yard before he woke up. He also ran over a bicycle, but we didn't think much about it at the time. Later on, one of the men working the wreck happened to see something hidden behind the bushes. It was a kid who had been delivering papers. The guy in the truck had run over the boy and the bike and didn't even know it."

I instantly felt the pain. My heart felt heavy, and I wanted to cry. Puzzled, I asked myself why I was so bothered by this. The heaviness eventually diminished, but it did not lift. We talked a little longer, then I excused myself for the night.

As I lay in my sleeping bag, I could still feel the inner hurt. Again, I wondered why. I have heard stories like this before and they had not affected me this deeply. Why this one? I prayed and fell asleep.

I woke with a jerk. It was four in the morning and still dark, but I was wide awake. I'd had a dream that troubled me—it was so real. I was talking to the husband of an old college girlfriend, and he was telling me how my relationship with her had hurt her and their subsequent marriage. I was crying, saying how sorry I was that my weakness had cost them both so much. She had cared deeply for me, but I had not treated her well. I had used her for my own selfish emotional and sexual fulfillment.

As I lay there thinking about what I had done to her, I began reflecting on my other relationships before marriage. I had been selfish and untrustworthy in many of them, giving love to get sex. But my heart ached the deepest as I realized I had done the very same thing to my wife. In the first years of our marriage, I had been unfaithful and never told her. As I reflected on my infidelity, I felt ashamed. Deep anguish over my sexual selfishness and especially at my adultery tore at me.

I now understood the intensity of my pain over the death of the paperboy. He was a symbol of my past, the shameful part of me that I had hidden in the bushes, never to be revealed.

The pain was coming from my shame and the fear of its exposure. I was now being found out. I could not keep hiding my past or my weakness any longer. I knew God was dragging it out of the bushes into plain sight for me to face.

Sleep would not return. My thoughts kept turning to the past. How could anyone be so uncaring as I had been? So deceitful, so shameless? By daybreak I knew I had to openly deal with my past. God was talking to me, telling me I needed to resolve this with Susan. My fears rose within me. What will she do? Will she leave me? I fought back the fears all day.

I arrived home late in the afternoon, and Susan immediately knew something was wrong. I was bothered and it showed.

"What's the matter, honey?" she asked.

I fumbled for words. What should I say? How could I think of hurting her even more by telling her? Hesitantly, awkwardly, the truth came.

"How could you?" she cried.

I did not have any answers, only pain for her pain; though no longer fearful, I grieved for the grief it caused her.

There was a lot of talking and prayer. A few days later she said to me, "Honey, I forgive you, but there is still a pain in my heart from all of this."

I knew what she meant. I took my hand and placed it over her heart and prayed aloud, "Jesus, I confess once again my sin before you and Susan and I ask you to graciously heal the wound of it in her life. Thank you, Lord, for your mercy and healing."

"I feel better. The hurt is gone!" Susan exclaimed.

The pain was left behind and my shame released. Somehow we felt closer than we had for years. Something between us had been removed.

Should You Tell?

My personal experience has encouraged me to advise many people to clear up their sexual past by sharing the truth of it with their spouse. However, I have also recommended to some that they not do it. As a pastor friend from Omaha reminded me, sharing your sexual past is very delicate territory. It is powerful—able to enrich your marriage or destroy it. Sharing the truth depends on where you are in your marriage and what God is showing you. That is why I have included this chapter. I want to offer guidelines for when to consider telling and when not to. I also want to offer you specifics on how to tell. Even when sharing your sexual past, there is wisdom on what to share and what not to.

Please realize that sharing a secret has its consequences. I had to accept the responsibility not only for having committed adultery but also for the pain that its revelation would cause. Revealing my adultery could have caused irreparable harm, potentially destroying my wife and our marriage.

After the last session of a seminar on sexual healing, a woman came to me in tears asking if she should tell her husband; in a moment of weakness, she had committed adultery with his cousin. Her husband was a big, strapping cowboy, well known for his physical prowess. He was also currently out of work and struggling with his self-worth, and their marriage was on shaky ground. She was afraid it would "kill" him to know. I concurred, encouraging her to seek in-depth advice from her pastor or a counselor before proceeding.

Sharing the secret, however, also has its benefits. Because of my confessing, Susan and I could enjoy better sex and a deeper level of intimacy. I was no longer afraid of the past, nor was I as afraid of Susan's rejection. The release of the shame created a new transparency in me, enabling me to be more honest with her and myself and with others about themselves. It also brought more mutuality to our sex life and greater fulfillment. This is a common positive change most report after dealing with sexual secrets and shame.

Why It May Be Important to Tell

Secrets and shame from the past hinder the oneness and intimacy that healthy marriages require. *Oneness* is the ability to come into unity and agreement. It is not sameness, but rather complementary differences unified in purpose, value, and direction. If two individuals are not in unity with each other, they will not be a healthy team for child-rearing, lovemaking, or any mutual task.

Intimacy is that profound experience of two souls touching, two spirits connecting, even two bodies joining. It is a powerfully enriching feeling that lessens our aloneness and draws us closer, making us more unified in emotion and direction. But intimacy is even more than this.

Intimacy speaks of the total baring of our innermost being—an outward transparency of our inward thoughts and feelings about who we are, who we were, and who we want to be. It is a total baring of self, a complete vulnerability. This total sharing of one's innermost thoughts, desires, fears, and dreams is the first component of intimacy. The second is total acceptance by the other person of what was shared.

The Scriptures refer to marriage as being one flesh, naked and not ashamed. For oneness to exist,

nakedness or total baring of one's self is necessary. So
is a lack of shame at what is shared, because the individual who shares the innermost being needs acceptance. So for intimacy to occur, the sharing must be
accompanied by the total acceptance of what was
shared. This is the foundation of all relationships . . . a
sharing of who we are, responded to with acceptance
by the other.

The shame we feel about our past is due to the
fear of unacceptance by those with whom we share.
As long as the fear is present, we will not totally bare
ourselves because we do not want to risk the rejection, which, in turn, compounds our shame. We will
wall off a part of our inner life from the view of others,
creating an obstacle to intimacy. At the same time, we
will also be resisting God's grace in the area of our
shame, because the partitioning off of our inner world
puts up barriers to God's work and help from others.
Our shame remains our own private possession, un-
touched by anyone—including God.

Paradoxically, it is the confession of our sinful-
ness that brings release to the shame. That which we
fear is what we must face in order to be healed. The
hidden territory will remain a stumbling block to us
and to intimacy until we are willing to risk its exposure. And uncleansed shame creates codependent and
compulsive sex.

The unfaithful wife will give her husband sex
even if she does not enjoy it because she secretly
knows of her unfaithfulness and fears his finding out.
It can be her way of penalizing herself, or of not facing
the fact of her dysfunctional sexuality and the pain in
need of resolve. Telling him of her infidelity or promiscuous past offers the potential for release. More than

anything else, confession faces the fear of rejection squarely in the face and breaks its power over her life. Her self-punishment and fear of rejection have been the underpinnings of her codependency. Her honesty cannot only bring freedom, but it can also bring the intimacy she so deeply craves.

Compulsive sex can also be fueled by shame because it breeds hopelessness and secrecy. When Ryan finally admitted to his hidden practices and past, healing came. Admitting to his compulsion also lessened the guilt and judgment his wife felt emanating from him, which greatly helped their relationship. The improvement in her self-worth encouraged her to approach him as an equal, enhancing intimacy and mutuality. His admission also invited counseling and prayer assistance that was previously unavailable. Tearing down the partitions that hid his secrets allowed God's grace and healing to enter.

When Not to Tell

Sharing your secrets and shame with your fiance or spouse can bring the freedom and intimacy every relationship needs and everyone craves. But what if the other person cannot accept your confession? Does that mean you should not tell? Probably. When confession could irreparably damage another, it is rarely wise to do so. The reason I say *rarely* instead of *never* is that God always has the last say. None of us can fully predict how another may react or how devastated the person may be by our confession.

Additionally, it is not totally advisable to trust our own perception of the situation, because our fear and shame will influence our judgment.

Restoring innocence
has to do with
removing the harm
of wrongful sexual
practices so that
true intimacy can
be experienced.
To do so requires
facing the pain of
our own secrets
and shame, as
well as handling
how they may
affect others.

Confessing our secrets and sin just to get things off our conscience is also not wise. Making another's cross heavier is not the answer to lightening our own.

Steps to Consider

For anyone with secrets or shame from the past, I recommend carefully considering the following steps in determining whether or not to share, as well as how to share.

1. *Pray first.* Do not do anything without prayer. Prayer will help you face yourself and pave the way to finding out whether this is really God's will for you at this time.

2. *If you are single and have past shame or secrets, you can gain freedom through sharing with a trusted counselor or pastor and asking him or her to pray for you.* In Alcoholics Anonymous the fifth step is sharing the results of a personal moral inventory with God and another person. Confession to another, when done in the right way, always seems to bring release.

3. *Do not tell your fiance, spouse, or lover anything without first having explored with another what you need to share and whether or not you need to share it at this time.* There is wisdom in counsel. Share with a trusted pastor or qualified counselor what you are considering. If this is really God's will, he will confirm it through wise counsel.

4. *Check your own motive.* Do you really want to follow God's leading in this, or are you just trying to get rid of your negative feelings by dumping them off

on another? Examination of our own heart is always a prerequisite to dealing with others.

5. *If you are engaged to someone, you owe a total confession before the marriage.* The marriage covenant is a commitment to totally love and accept the other until death parts you. One of the requirements of marriage should be the total baring of one's self to the other prior to marriage so that the other person can knowingly and fully come to terms with whether he or she wants to accept you "as is." Marriage should offer no surprises or hidden ghosts from the past. Much heartache can be saved when both covenant with a clear conscience and total transparency. Otherwise, you will defraud your partner.

6. *If the marriage is tenuous or the person fragile, go slowly.* An untimely confession can destroy a shaky marriage or hurt the other person. Make sure you get wise counsel and heed it. On the other hand, a cleansing of the past can be the exact thing needed to release the blockage and bring healing to the marriage. It can also be a part of God's dealing in the life of the fragile person, bringing him or her to the point of being broken in surrender before him. Either way, do not trust your emotions. Make sure you get counseling before proceeding.

7. *If the secret has to do with a current sexual affair or practice, you have no choice but to confess.* The bondage of your affair or secret practice cannot be broken without honesty. By keeping it secret, you will only delude yourself. The enemy always retains power in dishonesty. Second, the covenant of marriage de-

mands your honesty. Hidden affairs or shameful practices will cause confusion and distortions of perception on the part of the unsuspecting spouse. He or she will know something's wrong but will not really know what is happening. Keeping the sin hidden is like rubbing salt in a wound.

8. *If you are a minister of the gospel or in a helping profession, you have no choice but to confess.* The only question is when to confess and to whom. The secret shame will hinder your ability to help others. It distorts your perceptions and affects the message you offer. Ministers of the gospel will hinder the ability of God's Holy Spirit to work through them to touch others. Additionally, the secret territory will invite the harassment of the enemy through fear or temptation. Counselors or therapists also run the risk of being tempted to visit their bondage on their clients. Not dealing with private secrets and shame violates the trust others place in us, and that trust demands we live transparent lives before our God and others (see 1 Tim. 3, Titus 1:7–9).

9. *Choose the right place and the right time.* The right place and time should offer maximum privacy, providing room for the other person to emotionally respond. Make sure the kids are not around and you have hours of time, if need be. It is not wise to do this in front of others unless there is a concern for safety. Doing so may shame the person. You need to bravely face the one you have wounded unless you are so fragile and fearful, someone else's presence is needed to help you. If you fear violence and have still been counseled to tell, then find a safe place, making sure others are there to protect you.

10. *Be honest and contrite, but do not grovel.* This is a time of sharing and making amends. Apologize sincerely for that which requires it. Share openly what has happened to you and how it has affected you and the other person. It is healthy to feel compassion for the effects your past may have had on the other person and the marriage—especially if it has affected the marriage bed. Feeling the other's pain and grief is not wrong, neither is feeling your own. Make clear what your intent is in doing this. Express your hopes for a better, more honest and intimate relationship, your regrets for past wrongdoing, and your fears of their response. Tell them you need their forgiveness and acceptance.

11. *Do not share intimate details.* You do not want to offer details that will bring torment to the person; details such as how you had sex, where you had sex, and what you felt each moment during the event. Many lovers will want to know all this, thinking it will help them resolve what happened. I have never found it to help; rather, it hinders. Those who do want such detailed accounts are usually wounded individuals who will be more wounded by the telling. Rehearse ahead of time what to tell and what not to. Sharing who you were involved with is necessary, especially if it is someone the two of you may be in current relationship with. Your indiscretion has caused you to lose the privilege of relationship with that person.

12. *Give the one you confess to ample opportunity to process emotions and thoughts.* Do not expect an instant forgiveness and acceptance of what you have shared. It will usually take time to work through

the pain of your revelations. You need to allow that time. If the relationship remains distant for weeks and the person appears tormented or continues to be deeply offended, then counseling is necessary. The confession has touched other areas of unresolved pain, and the person will need help to resolve what is being felt.

13. *If everything does not work out as you planned, do not panic.* Hindsight is usually better than foresight. If you did this out of conviction, then give it time. The benefits may not be realized for months or even years. This exercise can bring instant change or it may take a long time. Do not look for a "quick fix." All things come with time when God has led the way.

My Concern

To be honest, I am concerned about offering this material. Some will not hear my message—they will either completely avoid what I said or they will go full steam ahead. But what I have recommended comes from seeing how others have done it in the right way as well as the wrong way. My concern comes from what I believe the Scriptures teach and what I know healthy relationships require. It also comes from the deep concern I have for people.

We are all fragile in our innermost parts. A wound of spirit is very difficult to bear. What I am offering is a chance to look at the wound of your own spirit and to cautiously and gently handle the wound of another. Relationships are always tested by the wounds we inflict upon ourselves and others, revealing the depth of our love and the power of the wounded condition. But wounds also remind us of our need for God. Only he can direct the way, smooth over the bumps, and repair the damage. He holds the future in his hands.

Restoring innocence has to do with removing the harm of wrongful sexual practices so that true intimacy can be experienced. To do so requires facing the pain of our own secrets and shame, as well as handling how they may affect others. There is a risk to handling wounds. It can make them deeper before they are healed, it can wound without a chance of healing, or it can bring greater release of intimacy and fulfillment. Only God knows the result. Trust him to guide you as he did me.

Chapter 11

LIVING WITH VICTIMS AND VICTIMIZERS

"*I* don't know what to do with my husband now that I realize he is a sex addict. Do I trust him, divorce him, or what?"

"I have recently remembered that my dad molested me. What do I do? I don't know if I can bear talking to him or seeing him again."

"What should I do about old lovers I have wounded? Do I need to make amends to them?"

"My wife was incestuously molested as a young girl. Now that I know what's behind our sex problems, what should I do?"

"What about my kids? Will they also have problems like me? What can I do to prevent it?"

Each of these questions has to do with managing the relationship issues that have resulted from the sexual wounding. It is hard to live with a sexually damaged spouse; the old wounds hurt you too. It is doubly hard to be sexually damaged and not have your spouse or loved ones understand. Coping with these issues takes generous amounts of wisdom, courage, and understanding.

In this chapter, I would like to offer advice on how

to deal with the other people in your life—those who affected you and those whom you are affecting. Hopefully, these guidelines will help educate and direct you and also challenge you to new ways of thinking and courageous ways of acting. However, I do not know your specific circumstance, and not every scenario possible has been covered. Before taking action, get support and counsel from a qualified therapist or pastor.

"My Wife Has Been Victimized"

"If I had my way, I would hang him up and skin him alive," was one husband's response to learning that his father-in-law had molested his wife when she was a child. He was hurt and angry, and he wanted revenge.

Anger and hurt are common reactions in husbands who learn of their wives' abuse or rape. They want to strike back at what has hurt them and their loved ones. But revenge, besides being biblically wrong, may cause the wives even more problems. When others react violently to a wife's or child's sexual wounding, it can make the wound deeper and the event even more traumatic. Violent or vindictive reactions cause more fear and shame for the victim who is already traumatized and wanting comfort and peace, not more pain and turmoil.

If a husband isn't supposed to strike back, then what can he do? The single greatest thing the husband of a wounded wife can do is offer his patience, care, compassion, and support. He will also need to take the initiative to find out what to do because his wife will be unable to convey all that she needs in order to recover. Discovering what to do may be especially dif-

It is hard to live
with a sexually
damaged spouse;
the old wounds
hurt you too. It is
doubly hard to be
sexually damaged
and not have
your spouse
or loved ones
understand.

ficult if she has blamed you for her problems or has defended herself too much, because you will not be able to trust her perceptions. That is why you may need to talk to other men, your pastor, or a qualified therapist. You will need their support in order to be able to support her.

But make sure you do not confuse support with counseling. Support does not mean trying to repair the damage yourself. She needs to find her own path to healing. You cannot unfold it for her or make her walk down it. Also, exert your love, not your power. Power is the ability to make a person do what you want done. Love makes her do what she thinks she should do.

Possibly the most difficult thing you will need to do is face your own wounds. Since marriage is a "one flesh" arrangement, what hurts one hurts the other. This is especially true of sexuality. Her inhibition, fear, or pain will limit your pleasure—you will pay the price for what happened to her and what she did about her hurt. But you need to accept her damage and commit yourself to loving her, even if your dream of great sex is never realized. Tears may need to be shed and God's healing touch invited. It can take time, but it will come if you seek it.

If you do not accept her limitations and accept the cost of it in your own life, you will remain angry and resentful. The bitterness will poison not only you but the entire relationship. It will also cause you to either give up on her and sex or continue to pressure and push for it, which is exactly the opposite of what she needs to recover. When sex has been forced upon a woman, any semblance of pressure or force from a husband causes her body and emotions to react as she did when violated. It kills all the pleasure and reinforces the problem. If you give up on her and sex, it only reinforces the deep-seated notion in her that says she is not worthy of love or attention, further encouraging her to give up on herself. Both reactions make things worse.

Helping her through her difficulty will test the very strength of your character. Character is the power to do what is right regardless of the cost. Can you commit to denying yourself in order to sacrificially love her? This is the challenge husbands of wounded wives face. For you, it may not be that difficult. For another, it will be the most difficult thing he has ever done.

If loving your sexually wounded wife is extremely difficult and you are having trouble accepting what has happened, then you need to examine your own investment in sex. It may be that sex is too powerful in your own life. Your lack of acceptance may be God's way of showing you your need for healing and change.

Finally, learn everything you can about sexual damage. If you join her in the quest for healing, it will be her greatest blessing and yours also. Many couples have grown closer and reaped better sexual fulfillment by accepting what is and prayerfully working together for what could be.

"What Do I Do with the One Who Has Hurt Me?"

If you were victimized by a dad, mom, uncle, friend, or mate, it is going to be difficult figuring out what kind of relationship you want to have, or even if you should have one with the offending person. However, these decisions may be crucial if you have daughters, sons, nephews, or nieces who could also be victimized. They can also be crucial to your healing.

Most victims of sexual abuse do not confront their abusers. Because the abuse usually takes place when they are young, it often does not get dealt with until adult years. By this time, however, everyone involved has gotten used to pretending the abuses did not happen, so the victims will feel as if they are causing an unnecessary "stink" by raising the issues or confronting the perpetrators. As one client shared with me, "It's better to let old dogs lie."

But *this is not true*. If you have been victimized, you may need to confront the person. The danger of not confronting that person will be your unbroken tendency to react to him/her in codependent ways. Victims of abuse are rarely honest with others; they either tiptoe around for fear of giving offense, or they are constantly offended, becoming angry and rebellious. This just sets them up for further rejection.

Honest, well-managed confrontation offers the opportunity to break the pattern of codependent relationships. It can give you freedom from the past and offer an opportunity for change. It also can protect you and others from continued abuse. Perpetrators rarely change unless the truth has been revealed and the wounds healed.

The following considerations may be helpful in figuring out what to do with the offending party.

1. *Pray before, during, and after confrontation.* Ask God for his wisdom on whether to confront, as well as how and when to confront. I have had clients excitedly share how God provided the perfect opportunity through prayers. Prayer and counsel are your safeguards. They will assist you in making the right decisions for the right reasons.

2. *If the person has not openly admitted to the abuse and has not shown clear signs of change, then you need to protect yourself and others from him or her.* A perpetrator cannot be trusted to have changed unless there is clear evidence to support it. Only open admission to the wrongdoing is the beginning evidence of a true change. Additionally, the person must seek help. Child molesters do not change with time. They change when they have been healed of the problem by dealing with themselves.

Also, do not let your fear of their reaction allow you to place your child or someone else's in danger. If you are challenged as to why you are keeping your child away, tell the truth. If other family members have children who may be affected, you need to confront the perpetrator, telling of your need to warn others unless you are provided evidence of the pattern having been changed.

Finally, do not totally trust your perceptions of whether or not they have changed. A qualified therapist can offer valuable insight. Demand an evaluation. A sincere individual who has changed will be willing to submit to such an evaluation. It may also be the excuse needed to ask for help.

3. *Do not confront until you are sure of your motives.* The purpose of the confrontation is not to punish, retaliate, get your abuser to love you or to rid you of anger. What you need to accomplish is to clear the air and the issue. You want the abuser to face the responsibility, and you want also to overcome your fear of the person. Confrontation breaks the power of the past over your life and provides the opportunity for amends to be made.

4. *Do not confront until you are emotionally ready*. You do not want to confront a perpetrator from a position of emotional vulnerability. Most abusers, at first, will deny they have done anything wrong and blame you for stirring up trouble. This means you must be strong enough to handle their rejection, denial, blame, anger, or punitive measures. If you are not emotionally ready, then you will knuckle under to the intimidation and end up mismanaging the confrontation and blaming yourself afterward.

5. *Do not confront until you have worked out exactly what you need to confront the person with*. This means that you want to be able to tell:

- what was done to you
- how it made you feel at the time
- how it has affected your life
- what you want now

Doing these four things in the confrontation gives a complete picture of the victimization to the abuser. It lets him or her truly know the result of those actions. Most perpetrators are oblivious to how their sin has affected others.

6. *You can use different means to confront*. A letter, a planned telephone call, or a face-to-face meeting can all accomplish your purpose. It all depends upon your level of comfort and what the situation dictates. With potentially violent perpetrators, it is rarely wise to confront face-to-face. If you must, however, make sure you have made provision for your safety by having the assistance of others immediately available—even the police, if necessary.

7. *Do not expect a victimizer to change.* You are confronting this person to bring healing to yourself and to call for accountability. He or she may not accept what you offer and may even become more entrenched in protests of total innocence. Do not be swayed by it. Stick to your guns and go on with your life. You can live without the approval, acceptance, or relationship.

8. *Allow your abuser to make amends, but don't expect too much.* To make amends means to make payment or reparation for the injury done. A penitent abuser can only make reparation by fully admitting to what he or she has done and apologizing for it. The abuser can't feel your pain, undo the damage, or heal you. A heartfelt apology can ease your pain but only God can fully remove it.

9. *If the perpetrator is deceased, bringing the truth out into the open can help.* Other individuals or family members may also have been abused. Your willingness to share can encourage others to seek the healing they need. Sharing openly about the abuse can also help you. Many victims doubt themselves and what happened to them, thinking it must have been all their fault or something conjured up in their imagination. The open sharing helps break the denial. Think carefully through how you will share and when to share. And remember, others may not want to face what you are telling them, so be emotionally prepared.

10. *Confront a deceased perpetrator through letters or role playing.* Being able to say how the abuse affected you and made you feel is a major benefit of

confrontation. Doing so in letter form or through role playing can help you let go of the anger and pain of being violated. It may also help you sort through your thoughts and feelings, leading to more resolution of the abuse. If neither of these means appeal to you, think creatively. A patient of mine wrote a story about her abuse. If neither of these means appeals to you, think sculptors, and writers have used their creative gifts to tell their story and complete their healing.

Reconciliation can come from a confrontation. But be aware that most confrontations do not bring reconciliation even though they provide healing. The confrontation exposes truth, but most perpetrators do not love the truth, which is why they need it so desperately. They also need less of our brand of loyalty and more of our honesty. It is the only hope for health. When truth is accepted, then reconciliation will occur.

Living with a Sexually Addicted or Compulsive Spouse

Among the most painful relationships I have seen are those where one of the spouses is addicted to sex. These persons may compulsively masturbate, frequent porno shops, visit prostitutes, or become involved with every attractive person of the opposite gender they find. They have an insatiable desire for sex and sexual experience. Living with such a spouse can be hell.

When they are not acting out their addiction with others, the sexually compulsive will be pressuring for sex. Their desire will prey upon the relationship like a voracious animal. Never quenched and never fulfilled, they will challenge your feelings of adequacy and prompt you to codependently give them the sex they demand, causing you to lose out on the love you need.

Sexually addicted spouses break and even trample the bonds of loyalty and trust in a relationship. Their infidelity causes a deep wound of spirit from which some have great difficulty recovering.

That does not, however, mean you should forsake an addicted mate. Even though there may be scriptural grounds for divorce, you still have a choice as to whether to remain in the marriage. If a sexual addict is working on a program of recovery, you may want to consider staying and working through the problems. Now, what do I mean by a program of recovery? To successfully work a program of recovery, a sexual addict must meet the following requirements:

1. *The addict must fully admit the addiction and its effect on his or her life and yours.* To fully admit means the addict is not in denial of the problem. He or she is able to describe the power the addiction has and recognize what it has done to his or her life and to others' lives. This is the first step of recovery from any addictive process.

2. *The addict must have a plan of recovery and be following it because the addict wants to, not because of being forced to.* Recovery from addiction takes time; therefore, a plan for change is essential. Is the addict attending support group meetings, counseling, or a recovery program? What does the addict think is needed? Has the addict willingly sought help from others? Has the addict worked out a plan of recovery in consultation with a professional or is he or she doing his own thing? Is freedom from bondage what the addict really wants?

Each addict must come face-to-face with these questions. If your addict has not, then doubt the sincerity. He may be powerless over the addiction, but he is not powerless to formulate a plan and stick to it. And sticking to the plan shows the level of personal commitment and desire and whether compliance is just to keep everyone happy or deliverance is truly wanted.

3. *Addicts must make themselves accountable to another for their addiction and their lives.* Because sexual addicts do not know how to conduct relationships in a healthy manner, merely stopping the addictive behavior will not teach one how to relate to you. They need the type of relational advice and training that accountability and discipleship require. They need another person to help them direct their relationships.

Also, sex addicts usually mismanage more than one area of their lives. Money, a commonly mismanaged item, is often used to support addictive behavior. Accountability can aid them in managing every area of their lives in a more healthy manner.

4. *The addict must be willing to make amends.* Recovery demands full responsibility. Making amends to those we have hurt indicates a willingness to accept responsibility for our actions. The anonymous programs of recovery have a step that requires listing all those to whom amends should be made. The next step requires the addict to make the amends, except where doing so would hurt another. Both of these steps are essential to recovery. If bitterness or indifference to the other is present, then healing will be hindered.

If you have victimized someone—a child, relative, girlfriend, or spouse—then you need to make amends in order to help your victim's healing. How to accomplish this will require wisdom and courage. If making amends might place you in legal jeopardy, consult an attorney first. But understand that you may need to follow through anyway. Someone else's life must take priority over your self-preservation when you have done the wrong.

5. *The sexual addict cannot be actively practicing the addiction.* Support sexual addicts, but do not live with one who is still into the addiction. The effects can be life-threatening. A client of mine has not only been betrayed, lied to, and blamed, but her addict-husband has also given her three venereal diseases. I have recommended separation and abstinence until it is clear he is on the road to recovery and not actively practicing his addiction. I also recommended a test for AIDS prior to resuming intercourse.

The reason I recommend abstinence is to help the addict break the power of the compulsive sexual practices. The planned period of abstinence has to be free from all sexual activity or stimulation in order to be effective.

Continuing an intimate relationship with a practicing addict is more a reflection of one's codependency than a demonstration of committed love. *Do not do it.* It only feeds the addiction and postpones the addict's recovery. The addict needs to learn how to live without sex in order for sex to be meaningful.

Make sure you have wise counsel and a lot of support. The wounds are deep and your need great. Many addicts do recover, but it takes time and a deep desire to be free. Trust in the Lord and ask for wisdom, and he will guide you.

"What about the Kids?"

What do we do to keep the kids from being affected by our problems? This question is the most frequently and fearfully asked. My first response is always the same: Do whatever you can to be whole and healthy. Healthy parents create healthy families and healthy kids. But healthy does not mean perfect. If compulsive sexual desire runs in your family, then your kids will probably struggle with it too. Weaknesses run in families; however, you can turn the tide by breaking their power in your life. Here are some practical things you can do.

- Learn all you can about healthy sex and sexuality.
- Talk to your kids about sex, but not in an emotionally incestuous way.
- Pray for your kids and their future mates.
- When they are old enough, share with them the battles and victories you have had.
- Keep the lines of communication open, and be quick to respond in caring ways to any negative event they have experienced.
- Guard over their relationships when they are young. Be available for counsel when they are older.
- Make information on sex available at the right stages in life.

These are but a few of the ways parents can help their children remain innocent. To whatever degree you have been able to face and change your unhealthy practices, it will be passed on to them. The other chapters in this book delineate specific developmental family issues that bear directly on sex and sexuality. Offer these to your kids to read.

My nineteen-year-old daughter has read some of the manuscripts for this book. Later, we talked about them. I asked her opinion and listened to her response. I have tried to keep the lines of communication open. Hopefully, she will be able to embrace both the pleasure and sacredness of sex. My prayer is that it will be less painful for her to learn than it has been for me.

As Iron Sharpens Iron

I know this may be hard to believe, but there can be benefits to living with a sexually compulsive husband or damaged wife or having to deal with a perpetrator. Proverbs 27:17 is a favorite Scripture verse of mine: "As iron sharpens iron, / So a man sharpens the countenance of his friend." I believe it takes the rubbing together of painful wounds and personal conflicts to sharpen us. Character comes from persevering through tribulation. As we are able to face the things and people in life that cause us to face ourselves, we can become more than we were. This has been true for me. I have also seen its positive effect in others. Living with a compulsive or damaged spouse has caused growth that could never have been actualized in any other way. Facing a perpetrator requires courage and inner resolve that may have otherwise gone undiscovered.

The old saying that some people "take lemons and make lemonade" can be true for you. Much of the progress made in healing victims of abuse has come from individuals such as Jan Frank, author of *Door of Hope*, who courageously faced her abuse, received healing, and went on to help others. You can do the same. Trust God to help you.

Chapter 12

HOW TO HELP RESTORE SOMEONE'S INNOCENCE

"*I*t was the most uncanny thing, Al. Right after discussing *Restoring Innocence* in our meeting, an old friend called, saying she had to tell someone and I was the only one she could talk to. I never would have guessed it, but her father had sexually molested her when she was a child, and it had all just come out in the open. She told me of the pain she felt and her thought of killing herself. I didn't know what to say. How do you help?"

All of us know someone who has suffered from sexual wounding. If we are not that someone, then it may be our daughter, son, neighbor, or the young wife from the Monday morning Bible study. Wounding has increased with our sexually permissive age.

A caring and gifted professional can help someone experience the healing needed. And a caring, sensitive, wise non-professional can help, even when a professional has not been able to. Nothing can supplant the healthy love and caring of another. So if you really care, you can help. However, misguided love can wound deeply. Helping requires both care and wisdom. The following guidelines can provide that wisdom in how to help. When in doubt, however, consult a professional who cares and knows how God heals sexual wounds.

Men for Men, Women for Women

Sexual attraction is powerful, and sexual counseling can stimulate attractions that otherwise would not develop. Because counselors and pastors have succumbed to the temptation of a sexual interlude with the person they were counseling, wisdom dictates that ideally men should help men and women should help women. Someone of the same sex often has better understanding and insight than someone of the opposite sex.

Also, few clients of the opposite sex can consistently handle the intimacy that sexual counseling produces. For women who have been abused by a man, it will be very difficult to trust a male counselor. For a male sex addict, the intimacy of counseling with a woman can provoke his desires even more. And, unfortunately, a codependent female client is inviting prey for a male counselor who will give her the affirmation and intimacy she desires in order to get the sex he wants. It is better to be safe than sorry.

Prepare Yourself

Dealing with sexual territory is difficult. It will make you face your own sexuality and unresolved sexual issues. The most helpful asset to helping others is to deal with your own unresolved territories first. Recovering alcoholics can help those still in bondage because they have faced their own weakness and realized God's strength and grace.

All of us know someone
who has suffered from
sexual wounding. If we
are not that someone,
then it may be our
daughter, son, neighbor,
or the young wife from
the Monday morning
Bible study . . . . Nothing
can supplant the healthy
love and caring of another.
So if you really care,
you can help.

Preparing yourself by studying and reading all you can about sexual problems and issues is also important. Knowledge helps to refine your people-helping skills. And don't just read the books, but underline them, study them, think about the material, and try to apply it in your life. This will give you additional insights into helping.

But do not underestimate the power someone else's problems may have on your own life. Hearing detailed accounts of abuse, perversion, and pain can deeply wound you. Make sure you are able to fully take on the other person's burdens without being overwhelmed. The ancient Judaic priests who offered daily sacrifices needed a laver to wash away the blood and sweat. You also need a way to release yourself from those burdens. Leisure time activities and prayer can help.

Make sure you have a routine time of prayer and devotion. Prayer prepares you for God's direction and enables him to work through you. Many times I have received the answer for a counseling session in prayer. Your time of devotion will also cleanse you from the worries and memories that can weigh you down. Also, a counselor is to carry God's message of hope and healing to another. If you are trying to give only your hope and message, it will not work.

Remain a Confidential Confidante

The Scripture says, "The words of a talebearer are as wounds, and they go down into the innermost parts" (Prov. 18:8 KJV). Sexual sharing is the sharing of one's most intimate thoughts, feelings, and beliefs. When you are privy to such, make absolutely sure that you do not share the confidence, or you can deeply damage the person. Your insensitive sharing of a sexual detail with another can, if found out, provoke a powerful, shameful reaction, encouraging the person to remain hidden and unhealed. Most wounded persons need encouragement to open up their pain. Your insensitivity will cost them. I cannot stress enough how important it is that you keep another's sex life confidential.

There are, however, two exceptions to this rule. I do not extend confidentiality to people when I know that to do so would endanger their lives or the life of someone else. A friend who threatens suicide because of his or her sexual wounding should immediately be reported to the police or a suicide prevention service.

The second exception is people who are victimizing another through abuse. Their compulsiveness is wounding another, and my silence would encourage its continuance. In such cases, I give them the choice of "coming clean," or else I take steps to uncover their abuse. This is not only a needed thing to do for the victim, but it also helps perpetrators get well by taking full responsibility for their actions. Do not ever try to help someone cover up violations of law or person. It only perpetuates the problem and keeps him or her from being healed.

Are You Accountable?

Professional therapists go through extensive training and supervisory experiences. They also participate in ongoing, multidisciplinary case staff conferences where a client's case is presented to other professionals for input and accountability. This assures that the client receives quality care. Pastoral counselors, prayer counselors, lay counselors, or helping friends also need training, supervision, and accountability.

If you are going to help another, make sure you have something to offer, and then make yourself accountable to someone who knows more than you. This is a safety feature for both you and the person you are helping. It will keep you honest and on track. When you work and pray for someone day after day, it is easy to become myopic. You can lose track of what is really needed. You may also unwittingly contribute to an unhealthy pattern of relationship. Accountability helps keep you focused.

If you cannot find someone to be accountable to who knows more than you about sexual counseling, then find someone you know who will be truthful. Accountability can be defined as keeping you committed to doing what you said you would do. A trusted person in authority can make sure you do what you say you are going to do. This type of accountability can also help.

Help Them, Do Not Try to Fix Them

Our Peace Corps made famous the motto of Helping Others Help Themselves. Your goal needs to be the same. There is a difference between helping another and fixing that person, and it lies in responsibility and control. If you take too much responsibility for others, then they will not take it for themselves. If they need you to take a lot of responsibility for them because they are unable to do so, then they need to be seen by a professional. Few of us can manage another's life in a healthy manner unless we have been trained for it. Additionally, you may end up in a position of control that is unhealthy for you, provoking your frustration or pride.

One of the telltale signs of trying to fix instead of help is how much credit you are taking. The more you see yourself taking credit, the less credit you are giving God and the person. This is pride, and we are all susceptible to its subtle lure. Also, if the person has become very dependent on you, then you are probably taking too much responsibility. Back off some, but do not just withdraw. That will further wound someone who is already hurting. Get someone you trust to help you work with their dependency.

Three Things to Always Do

Effective helping has three basic qualities. I call them the three things to always do. They are:

1. Listen more than you speak.
2. Always be lovingly truthful.
3. Help them face themselves and God.

For most people wanting to help another, these three guidelines will go a long way toward healthy helping. If you listen more than you speak, you will be more inclined to truly hear the person and less inclined to give bad advice. People need someone who will hear them out. Active listening skills will teach you how to ask questions that get to the heart of a matter. And the ability to ask the right questions is one of the most valuable tools a counselor has.

Questioning should begin with the here and now. Questions such as, What happened? How do you feel about it? How did you react?

Questioning should then proceed to there and then. Has this happened before? How did you feel when it first happened? What did you do then? Is there a pattern to your behavior?

These kinds of probing questions help get to the bottom of the problem. Examples are helpful, and your summarizing aloud what you heard can help the individual know you have truly listened.

The questioning cannot, however, be an interrogation. It has to be done gently and with sensitivity. Sexually wounded people need time and support to get the hurt out.

That is why you must always be lovingly truthful. Withholding the truth so you will not hurt feelings is really a self-protective device which does no good. People need to hear what others think. The only qualifications are that you (1) qualify what you say as *your* opinion, not God's; (2) offer your opinion, not force it; and (3) share everything in an attitude of love. Love balances out the truth, easing the pain of truth's cutting edge.

Your goal is to help the person face whatever needs healing and then to face God. Many do not receive healing because they look to people for it instead of God. But only God can deeply heal the wounds of spirit we all experience. Your job is to be a guide, helping to find the path to his healing, not yours.

With these three principles in mind, I would now like to share a model for healing sexual wounds. There is a risk in my sharing this model—you may think it works exactly the same way every time. But a model is only a prototype of the final product; it is used to guide one in working toward the final result. So use this model as a guideline, realizing that each person's path to healing will vary.

How to Heal Sexual Abuse in Women

1. *Encourage detailed explanation of exactly what happened and how the victim feels about it.* Shame is the hidden aftereffect of sexual abuse. Helping victims discuss what happened and how they feel about it, while giving them positive support and affirmation, will help defuse the shame. The post traumatic stress reaction is also defused when the person is given ample opportunity to discuss now what was forbidden then. Detailed discussion will help the victim face what happened and begin resolving it. If the person is reluctant, encourage but do not force. Opening up has to be the individual's decision, not yours.

2. *Encourage exposure of the situation and offending party.* As I have mentioned before, do not protect a perpetrator. Use wisdom when you encourage a victim to expose the situation, but do not support fear. When brought into the open, things may get shaken up, but healthiness is usually the result.

God honors open, caring, and honest confrontation. The hidden secrets of abuse fester with shame. Opening the sore is scary, but it also invites the light and air needed for inner healing.

3. *Walk the person through each memory with Jesus present.* Introducing Jesus into the equation will not only change perceptions, but his invited presence can heal. As the victim shares what happened with

Jesus, he or she should reveal innermost feelings, thoughts, and desires.

4. *Isolate the wrong judgments and vows they made as a result of the abuse.* Explore with them their inner perceptions of men, sex, intimacy, touching, foreplay, orgasm, oral sex, male sex organs, etc. The abuse can cause powerful negative inner attitudes in all these areas. If you pray and share, the wrong inner judgments and vows will surface. Some are quickly apparent, others are more subtle. Journaling can help isolate them. Comparing current thought with biblical truth can also reveal the judgments and empowering vows.

5. *Help them recant the wrong inner vows and judgments they have made and confess the truth.* Wrong inner evaluations are obstacles to healthy sexuality. Recanting them in prayer and confessing God's truth will begin to release the power they have over the victim. And affirming the truth will begin to imprint a new and healthier inner message. These newly adopted truths can be an effective weapon for dealing with lingering untruths.

6. *Discern any related areas of false and true guilt.* Victims are fraught with guilt, thinking the abuse was all their fault and that they caused it. Help them see that this is false guilt arising from their inability to control the situation well enough to avoid the abuse.

On the other hand, they may have made some mistakes or done things which put them in vulnerable situations, open to abuse. These are areas of guilt they must admit to, all the while not admitting to having caused the abuse itself. Whoever perpetrated the abuse is totally at fault for that. If the victim was seductive, foolish, or even disobedient to parents or others, the victim must take the responsibility for inappropriate behavior but not for the abuse.

Realize this is difficult territory that must be handled very carefully. If you are not expert enough at helping discern the difference between true and false guilt, get an experienced pastor or counselor's input before working through this with your friend.

7. *Help them confess any wrongdoing and receive forgiveness.* This step can release any true guilt. Because many need to hear the words "you are forgiven" before it becomes real, you may need to help by pronouncing forgiveness. If guilt still remains, though, look for other roots to the guilt. Other lingering events may still need examination and confession; for example, a woman who has never dealt with her prior promiscuity can feel guilty when raped, as if she deserved the rape. When the true guilt is resolved, the false guilt will leave also.

8. *Lead a victim to forgive the offending party.* Forgiveness is the key to releasing the past. However, the feelings of hurt, pain, resentment, or fear must be worked through first. Memories also need to be fully examined and released. All this takes time. Forgiveness is the goal, but it must not be used as a subtle form of avoiding working through the experience.

9. *Pray for release from the shame and hurt.* The shame and pain frequently disappear with prayer. As the Scriptures promise, the effectual prayer of a believ-

ing person can do a lot. So pray for cleansing from shame, and ask God to take away the stain the person feels because of the victimization. Also ask for the wound of violation to be removed and for a complete release from any emotional or spiritual attachment to the perpetrator. Your prayers will both invite God to heal and provide encouragement to the person, because it really does help to hear someone pray for you—even if it may be slightly embarrassing.

10. *Do not be in a hurry.* These steps take time and effort. I have seen God heal a long-standing memory of abuse in one counseling session, but I have also had to work for years in bringing healing to some abused persons. It can work both ways, depending upon the circumstances and the person.

Healing the Memories of Abortion

There is mounting evidence that abortion produces a post traumatic stress reaction in women, especially those women who prize children and life. I have had numerous women unexpectedly break into tears when we talk of past abortions. Not dealing with the loss and guilt of the abortion causes a delayed reaction. It may also create or contribute to problems ranging from depression and fatigue to inhibited sexual desire and codependent sex.

To help a woman receive healing for an abortion, follow the above listed steps. Also encourage her to realize she may need to mourn the loss of the child just as though the child had been born and then died. The normal pattern of grief applies to abortion. She will have to work through the stages of denial, anger, depression, bargaining and guilt before resolution comes.

A good resource is the book *The Morning After: Help for the Post-abortion Syndrome* by Terry L. Selby.

Encourage the woman to name the baby. Doing so gives identity and breaks through the denial, allowing the grief and comfort to come. Have her offer the baby to Jesus, asking him to forgive her and further asking him to offer her amends to the child. These steps can bring powerful healing and release to miscarriage as well.

Healing Compulsive Sexual Behaviors

Many of the same principles for healing sexually abused women apply to healing compulsive sexual behaviors. I will briefly list the principles, amplifying on the additional steps one must take.

1. *The person must admit the compulsion.* Any compulsive behavior requires full admission to the problem before change can occur.
2. *The individual must uncover and resolve any physical or emotional abuse experienced because of another.* Abuse leads to abuse, so healing for the prior abuse will break the power of the compulsion.
3. *Help the person uncover and resolve any incidents of defrauding.* Resolution of the defrauding requires mourning what could or should have been, plus letting go of the dream of attaining that which was withheld. The person may need to grieve the loss before acceptance and healing come.
4. *Have the person recall the first sexual experiences, inviting Jesus into them and recanting unhealthy initial imprints.*
5. *The person must fully reveal and make*

amends, where possible, for any sexual violation of another. Healing comes as personal responsibility is fully embraced.

6. *Help to uncover inner judgments and vows made regarding sex, sexuality, women, men, etc.*

7. *Help your friend recant wrong judgments and vows and confess the truth.*

8. *Assist the individual to pray for release from any emotional or spiritual attachment still felt for others, including pornographic images.*

9. *Have the person invite Jesus into any haunting memories that come from the past or from fantasies. He will bring a change of perception and power.*

10. *Pray against the compulsion, taking authority over it in the name of Jesus.* The sexual addict who is released from the compulsion is experiencing the same gift of release that an alcoholic experiences when the compulsion to drink is gone. Both compulsions are spiritually empowered; their release is a free gift from God actualized through surrender and prayer.

11. *Keep them accountable.* It is easy to fall off the straight and narrow unless someone is routinely checking and keeping them accountable to their stated plan of recovery.

Each of the models I have presented is a way in which I have seen both professional and lay individuals help sexually wounded persons. By applying these steps in your own life, you will be better able to help another. As with the last step of Alcoholics

Anonymous, which requires the person to share what he or she has learned with other afflicted alcoholics, sharing our wholeness with others in need continues our healing while they are being healed.

What I have offered to you is what I have experienced and witnessed in the lives of countless others. As God restores your innocence, offer this hope to others in need.

Chapter 13

BELIEVE IN THE GOD WHO HEALS YOU

*I*t's hard to believe that God invades the ordinary events of life to heal us unless you have witnessed it firsthand or heard the testimony of someone else. I feel privileged to have prayed for many wounded women and men and to have seen God heal broken hearts, release painful memories, and redo unhealthy imprints. When I share this fact with others, there is always interest. Frequently, there is skepticism. Many doubt God's personal intervention yet curiously hope it is true. If you are struggling with whether God will heal you or someone you love, I hope the following story will encourage you.

I met Bob at a writers' conference. As we talked, he shared a deeply moving story . . . a true story of God's direct intervention in his life. I have kept his written account, knowing it was meant for this book. It describes what I have witnessed countless times— God's healing touch.

Bob's Story

I enjoyed one of the first cool mornings of fall as I sat outside Swensen's restaurant waiting for my friend

Janie to arrive. It seemed so strange to be part of her life once again. So many years filled with so many different feelings and events had become part of our history. Now, after several years of little contact, we picked up our friendship.

As she entered the restaurant patio, she smiled and waved in her familiar, eager manner. She had a way about her that was unfailingly appealing to men. There was something of a vulnerable little girl, mixed with a soft and seductive woman that seemed to play some version of every man's fantasy.

We sat that morning and looked back on a friendship that spanned ten years and an incredible number of relationships. We had been friends, lovers, estranged lovers, and friends again. I had been her confidant, her boyfriend, her suitor, but most of all, always her friend.

We brought many things to the breakfast table that cool morning. I was newly married after several years as a single parent. She was recently out of a job and recovering from a destructive relationship. We laughed and sang a chorus of "Send in the Clowns." One of us had always been "up in the air" while the other was "down on the ground." But on this patio on this particular morning, it all seemed proper and right.

We talked of her life over the past few years. She spoke of a continuing pattern of punishing herself by somehow choosing relationships and situations that were unhealthy and destructive. George was the latest in a long line of men who were attracted to her beauty but ended up using and abandoning her. Under the surface tranquility of that morning, I could sense the deepening tragedy of her life. She was thirty-five years old, beautiful, but alone. She had come from a glamor-

ous public profession but now her professional identity was in question. She seemed unable to find the
self-esteem and motivation necessary to break out of
destructive patterns.

My awareness of these underlying factors was
only part of the picture that morning. I was also aware
of the mysterious chemistry that was once again at-
tracting me to her. The vulnerability she presented
was working its spell on me, as it had so many times
before. We talked and laughed and parted, agreeing to
meet again for breakfast and continue to rebuild our
friendship.

Danger signals flashed in my mind all the way to
the office. There was more than friendship at work
here. I was being seduced, not consciously or deliber-
ately, but nevertheless seduced. And I was willingly
participating in the process.

Too much was at stake. We met again at Swensen's and talked openly about what was going on. Why
was this pattern repeating itself? What was operating
between us? Openly acknowledging the dynamic was
like defusing a bomb. The dynamic still existed, but
its explosive potential was removed. We were able to
continue our friendship on relatively safe ground.

As the months passed, Janie began to reveal her
fears in more detail. One morning she reached a point
where tears flowed as if they would never stop. Finally,
between sobs, she quietly spoke of an incident that
occurred when she was twelve years old. An adult uncle had sexually molested her during a summer vaca-
tion with her parents at a lake. Two incidents had
taken place—the second at a boat dock while she and
her uncle waited for her parents to arrive.

Her sobs gradually quieted. "I've never told anyone that before, ever," she whispered. "I knew he was

doing something wrong and awful, but I didn't know how to stop it. I told my parents later and they were very angry at *me!* But the really awful part, Bob, is that even though I was frightened and sick about it, I remember that it felt good. Ever since then, a day doesn't go by without the image of that incident on the dock replaying in my mind. Every day for twenty-three years I have been reminded of what a shameful woman I am."

"Why are you a shameful woman?"

"Because I let it happen and because it felt good."

I held her hand quietly as the minutes ticked away. I was completely helpless. The tragedy of an innocent young girl carrying such guilt for so many years was appalling. No wonder she punished herself in relationships. No wonder she was sexually confused.

I continued to grope for words. But words could not heal the deep places of her soul that were so grievously wounded. No wise counsel came from my mouth. Not even words about the comfort of God. I had no comfort, other than my friendship, to give.

Alone in the quiet of my car, I fought my helplessness. My relationship with God was distant and lacked power. I was deeply embarrassed by my own repressed feelings of continuing attraction to Janie. How could I even think of being another in the long line of abusers in her life?

Our friendship continued. She began a new counseling relationship with a psychologist who enjoyed a good reputation in the area. Her life settled somewhat but continued its gradual slope downward. I continued to grope along my own dimly lit spiritual path, trying to be a husband, father, and teacher—all with little strength from God.

February found me a reluctant participant in a men's retreat for three days. The experience was called "Walk to Emmaus" and had been highly touted by those well-meaning friends who drove me crazy with their spiritual enthusiasm. To finally silence them, I set aside the three days.

My reluctance vanished as the first evening began with silence and prayer. I knew with a certainty that seemed to spring from a secret place deep within me that I was here for a purpose. I meditated on the stations of the cross and felt a quiet begin to seep into my noisy mind. My watch was confiscated, and I slept that night with no way to count the passage of the dark hours. I woke to more silence and an anticipation of a voice that would somehow speak during the days ahead.

The silence was broken with breakfast, and I entered a sharing and learning experience with forty other men. Each hour brought new surprises of love and caring from old friends and from people I had never met. I was swept along on a quiet journey of discovery.

Saturday evening we approached a service of healing. The noise returned to my mind. I revived my familiar skepticism that had been dormant for two days. Healing implied an intervention of God in ordinary events. For all my quiet renewal, I was not ready to play that game. But as I approached the altar and knelt before my friends, I knew clearly that there was one healing that was needed above all others. I whispered my request that my friend Janie be healed.

"Is there more?" asked my friend.

I quickly explained her past and her need for new life and healing.

"Yes," said my friend, "and is there more?"

Everything had to be laid on the altar for healing. My friend's insight allowed no games to be played. I was being pressed against the wall, and I had no choice but to quietly lay before God my own participation in Janie's wounds and my willingness to be healed as well.

"Dear Jesus," my friend began, as my other new friends of the past two days laid their hands on me, "hear our prayer for the healing and release of our sister Janie."

A drop of oil was tenderly caressed on my forehead. "And for the healing of our brother Bob." Another drop of oil was applied. "By the power of your Spirit." Another drop. "All praise and glory to you, our Father, through Jesus, our Lord. Amen."

The retreat continued amid a spirit of peace and love for all participants. I felt quiet and renewed as I sat at the closing ceremonies. I felt a new sense of release and purpose. The healing ceremony was a beautiful memory of personal psychological release that I was sure would be good for me.

Perhaps, I thought, this is the value in healing ceremonies. My deepening quiet and my old skepticism were once again settling in side by side.

The following Tuesday I had my weekly breakfast with Janie. She entered the restaurant with the usual smile and wave. I was anxious to tell her of my retreat and the beginning steps of quiet and peace I had taken, but before I could begin, she started to talk in a newly confident voice.

"Bob, the most wonderful thing has happened. Saturday evening I went to bed early and woke up about eleven. I had a vivid image of the incident on the dock. I assumed that it was the usual fantasy and memory that I've lived with for so long, but as I visualized it, it changed. A figure walked out on the dock and sat down between my uncle and me. It was Jesus, Bob, and he looked so loving and strong. He said to me, Janie, nothing is going to happen to you. I will protect you.'

"He did, Bob! He did protect me! Jesus just sat there and talked with me and laughed with me, and my uncle was entirely out of the picture. All I saw was Jesus. He told me that I was good and clean and that I could forget this incident now.

"Bob, I have been healed. That incident has not come to mind since."

"What time did you say this happened?" I asked quietly.

"About eleven o'clock."

Eleven o'clock! Exactly the time the oil was being placed on my confused forehead.

I rejoiced with Janie, inwardly trying to process our experience and somehow salvage my skepticism. But the decisive battle had been won. I could no longer doubt God's healing.

In the years since this incident, Janie has been totally free of her wound of self-shame. She has gone on to new struggles and healings in her journey with God, and I have continued on my own journey. We remain close friends. We are witnesses to the power of God to release, to heal, and to love in ways that are beyond our own powers of manipulation and need. Trusting in his healing presence, I continue to bring my wounds to the altar to be healed.

Obstacles to Healing

Bob's story has a number of lessons for us. Janie's recurring memory of the abuse is common, as is the experience of shame because of the pleasure she felt. This is why early childhood experiences of abuse can be so confusing. The girl or boy frequently experiences both aversion to the experience and physical sensations of pleasure but does not know how to sort through the experience to arrive at a healthy resolution.

Janie's promiscuity is also a frequent result of abuse. Coupled with family patterns of dysfunction, the abuse triggered her codependent and, at times, compulsive practice of seeking love through sex. Her beauty intensified the problem because men were easily attracted to her, giving her the love she sought to get the sex her seductivity promised.

Healing of her memory came through God's direct intervention. Remember, though, that it came *after* she had faced the memory through counseling and prayer. It also came as Bob faced his contribution. Realize that God's direct intervention often comes after the soil has been plowed, the seeds planted, and the crop watered. We must be ready to be healed. The obstacles are within us, not him.

I believe there are two main obstacles to God's healing. The first is not recognizing or admitting to our wounds. A heartfelt admission of our need for healing invites his compassion and care, and it also prepares us for healing. Many think they must carry the burden of their wounds alone. But self-sufficiency rules out God-dependency. You cannot rely on yourself to fix yourself if what you need is God's healing.

Emotional, even spiritual, healing requires honesty and vulnerability on our part. We need to admit that we cannot fix it. We need to open our inner being to his presence. This is why many a path to healing has been oiled by tears. Our being broken opens the door and proclaims our need.

There must also be an invitation for him to heal. God's Holy Spirit—a Spirit of comfort, wisdom, and grace—is the agent of healing. As someone once said, "The Holy Spirit is a gentleman. He will not come in unless invited." Even if skeptical, one must request God to heal. Bob was wrestling with his skepticism, but he still admitted to his need and asked God for healing. Janie was also seeking healing. Do not be too proud to ask.

Which brings us to the second obstacle: pride. Bob needed to humble himself before his friend and ask for healing. Make sure your insecurity, pride, or skepticism is not keeping you from being set free. In Alcoholics Anonymous, each recovering alcoholic faces a challenge: "Are you willing to go to any lengths necessary to be healed?" Sexually wounded individuals need to take whatever step is necessary to having their innocence restored, or they will continue to live in shame and dysfunction.

Sometimes, pride is even a mask for shame. Many are not healed because they are too embarrassed or ashamed to take the necessary steps of opening their inner life for healing. Have courage. Start slow. You only need to take one step at a time . . . but you must take the first step of admitting to yourself, another person, and God your need for help and healing.

The Touch That Heals

Janie's experience is not unique. Many women in our culture have been sexually abused or used. Many men also have difficulty with compulsive sexual de-

_____

In my distress I cried to the Lord,

And He heard me. . . .

It is better to trust in the Lord

Than to put confidence in man.

(Ps. 120:1, 118:8)

sires. Paradoxically, they frequently are attracted to each other. She will give sex to get his love and he will offer his love for sex. Sex may be good at first but it will not last that way for long. One will want more sex while the other less. Neither sees their need for healing and hope diminishes with every new attempt at fulfillment. Her codependent pattern of sex is being fueled by his compulsive sexual desire, making the climate for healthy relationship difficult to find—married or single.

The answer lies in overcoming events from the past that are controlling the present. This is true, whether or not you've been seriously abused or mildly wounded. These self-defeating practices are symptomatic of deeper unfulfilled needs, pained memories and unhealed wounds. Hurtful family legacies and past love experiences are contributing to current difficulties.

If you face yourself and then face God, he will heal the memories and wounds hindering your intimacy. Having the faith to believe he will help and heal is the challenge. My faith has been increased by my own experiences of healing and the countless times I have seen him intervene in the ordinary events of life to heal others. Believe in the God who heals you, for indeed,

> He heals the brokenhearted
> And binds up their wounds . . .
> Great is our Lord, and mighty in power;
> His understanding is infinite. (Ps. 147:3, 5)

His touch is available to remove the harm, heal the hurts, and restore your innocence.

Appendix

CONFIDENTIAL QUESTIONNAIRE-INVENTORY

*T*his confidential questionnaire-inventory is designed to help you explore intimate areas of your sexual practice and past so that you can experience discovery and recovery.

The questions are in-depth and personal, so prayerfully consider each one before you answer. Some may require special thought, time, or feedback. The more in-depth and detailed your response, the greater the potential for healing and change.

A word of caution: As you answer some of these questions, your feelings may range from anger and offense to discomfort and shame. Listen to what they are telling you. Those feelings signal the areas in need of further resolution or healing.

If the emotions become too powerful, *STOP!* Pray and continue again at a later time. You may need to discuss and work through the feelings with another person. But do not put them off forever. Healing comes as you face and work through the emotions and issues one at a time.

The following definitions and examples are provided to assist you in completing the inventory.

Judgment: An inner evaluation of a person or situation that is factually wrong or comes from a wrong inner motive.

Vow: An inner promise or pledge to one's self that binds one to behave or respond in a certain manner.

Example: A teenage girl on her first big date is taken home early by a neighborhood friend because her date had rejected her for not playing sexual games with him.

Her judgment: Men only want me for sex.

Her inner vow: I'll never trust men again.

This young girl is not able to see how it is not true that all men only want her for sex; she is blind to the friend who helped her by taking her home—a neighbor boy she had grown up with. Her vow to never trust men again causes her to make self-defeating decisions in the future. The vow and judgment come from her unresolved embarrassment and the wound of rejection she experienced.

Sexual Offenses

The following set of questions will help you explore how others may have wounded or offended you. Do not minimize what may have happened by saying to yourself that the event was no big deal. Instead, examine it and see what it tells you about your sexual responses today.

1. Have you ever been seduced or sexually used? If so, how and by whom?
2. Have you ever been sexually molested? If so, when, how, and by whom?

3. Have you ever been the victim of rape, date rape, or incest? Explain what happened.

4. Have you ever been wounded by a spouse through:

   - masturbation?
   - adultery?
   - homosexuality?
   - previous sexual sin?
   - lack of sexual response?
   - sexual rejection?
   - pornography?
   - other?

5. Have you ever been sensualized (sexually stimulated through sight, word, or deed before you were ready to handle this) by a parent or relative? By whom?

6. Have you ever been subjected to the probing eyes of a peeping Tom? When and where?

7. Have you ever been abused through sexual means? If so, by whom? What happened? When and where did it take place?

8. Have you ever been sexually embarrassed by someone by accident or by plan? When? Where? By whom?

9. Have you ever been sexually pressured until you finally felt like you had to give in? By whom? How many times?

10. List the names of all who have sinned against you.

11. How did you respond to their offenses? Outwardly? Inwardly?

12. Have you *specifically* forgiven each of them? Why or why not?

13. Have you been prayerfully released of the sexual bonding you had with each of these people?

14. As a result of their acts against you, what

negative inner vows and judgments have you made about:

- men?
- women?
- sex?
- marriage?
- God?
- other?

15. Have you totally recanted your wrong inner vows and judgments?

16. What did you do, if anything, that contributed to their acts against you?

17. Have you taken full responsibility for your contribution?

18. Have you taken full responsibility for the wrong ways, if any, you reacted?

19. Have you been totally healed of the effects of their acts against you and your own wrong response? Why or why not?

Personal Practices

This set of questions will help you examine your own personal practices. An essential step to healing and recovery is the fearless completion of our own inventory of sexual practice. This will help you face your guilt and release your shame.

1. Have you participated in premarital sex? If so, how many times and with whom?
2. Have you participated in premarital petting or sexual touching? If so, how many times and with whom?
3. Have you ever seduced someone sexually in

order to get emotional needs met? If so, how many times and with whom?

4. Have you ever seduced someone for what seemed to be totally sexual needs? If so, how many times and how?

5. Have you taken responsibility for your seduction and asked forgiveness? Why or why not?

6. Have you ever pushed too hard for sex, committed incest, rape, had sex with a child, or sexually molested someone? How many times and with whom?

7. Have you confessed this? Made amends? Received counseling? Why or why not?

8. Have you ever viewed pornography? If so, how often and what kind?

9. Do you still battle with pornography and unwholesome thoughts?

10. Have you ever masturbated? If so, how many times and over what span of time?

11. Do you still battle with masturbation?

12. Does your spouse know about your background (and current practice) with pornography and masturbation? Why or why not?

13. Have you ever participated in homosexual activities (experimental or otherwise)? If so, how many times and with whom?

14. Have you ever participated in voyeuristic activities, i.e., peeping Tom? If so, how many times and with whom?

15. Do you feel totally cleansed of these experiences, or are you still battling temptation?

16. Have you ever committed adultery? If so, how many times and with whom?

17. Have you confessed your adultery to your

spouse and asked forgiveness? Why or why not?

18. Have you ever had sexual experiences with a prostitute? If so, how many times?

19. List the names of all the people you have been sexually involved with outside of marriage through adultery, fornication, premarital sex, prostitution, etc.

20. Do you still think of them? Are you emotionally or spiritually attached to any of them? If so, why?

21. Do you carry shame or guilt over any of these past sexual experiences?

22. Have any of these experiences wounded you? How?

23. Have you been totally healed of the effects of your experience? Why or why not?

24. What negative judgments or inner vows have you made about sex, marriage, or members of the opposite sex because of your past experiences?

25. Have you totally recanted the wrong inner vows and judgments?

26. Did any of your past practices violate your conscience or God's law? Have you asked forgiveness? Why or why not?

27. Do you feel forgiven? Why or why not?

Sexual Response

The following questions relate to your sexual response patterns. They survey the four different phases of sexual response, starting with initiation of sex and ending with unwinding after sex.

If you are currently active, answer the questions

relative to current practice. If you are not currently active but have been in the past, then answer as they relate to past experience. The questions will help you evaluate your sexual responses, pinpointing areas of strength and areas in need of change.

Initiation of Sex

1. During the past month, how many times have you had intercourse? _____ times. How many times would you like to have intercourse? _____ times.
2. Is there a conflict in how frequently you would like intercourse?
3. During the past month, how many times have *you* initiated intercourse? _____ times. How many times has *your spouse* initiated intercourse? _____ times.
4. Is there a conflict about who initiates sex?
5. Is the way you usually initiate intercourse acceptable and pleasing to your spouse?
   ☐ Yes ☐ No
6. Is the way your spouse initiates intercourse acceptable and pleasing to you?
   ☐ Yes ☐ No
7. Do you usually resist initiation of sex or do you positively anticipate it?
8. What hurt or resentment do you have regarding your partner's initiation of sex?
9. What has kept you from totally forgiving him or her?
10. What fears do you have about sexual initiation?
11. Are any of your fears or resentments tied to the distant past or other loves?

12. What judgments or vows have you made regarding the initiation of sex?
13. What has kept you from completely releasing your wrong vows and judgments?

Sexual Arousal and Pleasuring

1. Are you easily aroused or do you find difficulty in becoming aroused?
2. What do you or your partner do that makes arousal easier and better for you?
3. What interferes with your arousal?
4. What does your partner want you to do to make arousal better for him or her? Do you do it? Why or why not?
5. What do you do, if anything, that makes arousal and pleasuring offensive to your spouse?
6. Is foreplay exciting and pleasurable for your spouse, or is it awkward or unpleasant?
7. Is foreplay exciting and pleasurable for you, or is it awkward or unpleasant?
8. Do you have any fears about foreplay?
9. Are there any aspects of your foreplay that create conflict?
10. What resentments or hurts do you still carry against your spouse in the area of foreplay?
11. What has kept you from totally forgiving?
12. What is your time of foreplay?
    ☐ Short (5–10 minutes)
    ☐ Medium (25–30 minutes)
    ☐ Long (60 minutes)
13. What dictates the length of your foreplay?
14. *For men to answer.*
    a. Have you ever had difficulty with obtaining or maintaining an erection?

    b. How many times has it happened?

    c. Have you consulted a physician?

    d. Have you been successful in overcoming any anxiety associated with sexual performance? Why or why not?

    e. How have you handled your fears of failure?

    f. Do you have any deep resentments toward your wife?

    g. Is she domineering, critical, or controlling with you?

    h. What judgments and vows have you made against her?

    i. What has kept you from releasing them?

    j. Do you have any guilt or shame from your past?

15. *For women to answer.*

    a. Do you have difficulty accepting your body?

    b. Do you see the vagina as wholesome, clean, and beautiful?

    c. What judgments and vows do you have against your female parts?

    d. Do you appreciate your husband's penis as a creation from God?

    e. Can you be "naked and not ashamed" with your husband?

16. Do you enjoy or dislike oral sex

    a. performed on you?

    b. performed by you?

17. Does your spouse enjoy or dislike oral sex

    a. performed on him or her?

    b. performed by him or her?

18. What is your conviction (not preference) regarding the role of oral sex in your marriage?

19. Is there a conflict or difference of convictions between you and your spouse regarding oral sex? How have you solved it?
20. What judgments or vows have you made about:

    • pleasuring your spouse?
    • being pleasured by your spouse?

21. What has kept you from releasing those vows and judgments?
22. What position do you prefer for intercourse?
23. What position does your spouse prefer?
24. Is there conflict regarding positions?
25. Is there variety in your positions? Why or why not?

Orgasm

1. Do you reach orgasm:

    • regularly or always?
    • periodically?
    • never or seldom?

2. Are you satisfied with the frequency of your orgasmic response? Why or why not?
3. Does your spouse reach orgasm:

    • regularly or always?
    • periodically?
    • never or seldom?

4. Are you satisfied with the frequency of your spouse's orgasmic response? Why or why not?
5. Do you reach orgasm together? Separately?
6. Have you tried to increase the frequency of your orgasm?

7. Check which of the following methods you have tried to increase orgasm:

   - Kegel exercise
   - Extended pleasuring
   - "Erotic" lovemaking
   - Pornography
   - Clitoral stimulation
   - Oral sex
   - Masturbation
   - Vibrators or other devices

8. Have your attempts resulted in:

   - Success?
   - Failure?
   - Anxiety?
   - Hopelessness?

9. Did you get clear spiritual direction from God on what to try before you tried? Why or why not?

10. Have the methods you have used violated your conscience or biblical morality?

11. Have you confessed or repented?

12. Have you consulted a doctor or a counselor?

13. What kind of orgasmic response do you usually have?

    - Mild
    - Medium
    - Intense

14. What kind of orgasmic response does your spouse usually have?

    - Mild
    - Medium
    - Intense

15. What judgments do you have about:

- letting go?
- loss of control?
- wild abandonment?
- submission?

16. What has kept you from releasing those vows and judgments?
17. Have you made your orgasmic response a subject of continual prayer and encouragement? Why or why not?

Relaxing and Unwinding after Sex

1. Are you quick to get up and get going or do you turn over and go to sleep? What about your spouse?
2. Check how you feel after sex.

- Affectionate
- Warm
- Glowing
- Tender
- Tired
- Irritated

- Anxious
- Embarrassed
- Ashamed
- Guilty
- Other

3. If there are any negative feelings, do they come from your distant past or other lovers?
4. What vows and judgments do you still carry from the past?
5. What has kept you from releasing them?
6. Do you have difficulty accepting or dealing with the fluids or wetness of sex?
7. Do you feel the need to clean up right away?
8. Where does the root of that discomfort come from?

9. Is there fear of being relaxed with your spouse, being "naked and not ashamed"?
10. Where does the root of that fear come from?
11. Have you dealt with that as a fear?